1000 Stranger Things Quiz Questions

The Ultimate Stranger Things Trivia Challenge

GW00469611

Mike Steed

CONTENTS

115 - 350-399
118 - 400-449
121 - 450-499
125 - 500-549
128 - 550-599
131 - 600-649
134 - 650-699
137 - 700-749
140 - 750-799
144 - 800-849
148 - 850-899
151 - 900-949
155 - 950-1000

INTRODUCTION

The book that follows contains one thousand questions all about the amazing Netflix show Stranger Things. Your knowledge on all aspects of the show will put to a severe test in the many questions which follow. The questions cover a range of subjects - from the cast, to plotlines, to characters, to pop culture references, and so on. So, put down that waffle and walkie-talkie, dim the lights, and prepare to take on the ultimate Stranger Things trivia challenge!

QUESTIONS

(1) What are the names of the two brothers who created Stranger Things?

(2) What is the name of Hopper's late daughter?

(3) What is the name of the trailer park where Max and Eddie live in Stranger Things 4?

(4) Who was the first character in the show to use the term 'Upside Down'?

(5) What type of computer does Dustin's girlfriend Suzie own in Stranger Things 4?

(6) Nancy's best friend in season one is the doomed Barb. What is Barb's full name?

(7) In the first episode of Stranger Things 3, the kids are smuggled into the Starcourt Mall cinema by Steve to watch a horror movie. What is the name of the horror film they watch?

(8) In which year was the board game Dungeons & Dragons invented?

(9) What is the name of the popular cheerleader who is killed by Vecna in the first episode of Stranger Things 4?

(10) In season four, Eleven and the Byers family move to California. What is the name of the town they move to?

(11) What is the name of the primary typeface used for the Stranger Things art and its title sequence?

(12) Stranger Things was not the original title of the show. What was it originally going to be called?

(13) How many members of the Stranger Things cast have appeared in the Alien movie franchise?

(14) Samantha Stone is the punkish girl that Jonathan chats to at the Halloween party in season two. Jonathan takes her for a KISS fan but turns out to be wrong. Who has Samantha really come dressed as?

(15) In the Stranger Things 4 finale, Eddie and Dustin stage an impromptu concert in the Upside Down to distract the DemoBats. What is the name of the song that Eddie plays on his guitar?

(16) Which character has the most lines in season one of Stranger Things?

(17) Eleven famously loves Eggo waffles in Stranger Things. In what year were Eggos invented?

(18) Stranger Things takes place in the town of Hawkins in Indiana. Which county of Indiana is Hawkins located in?

(19) What country does Finn Wolfhard come from?

(20) The name of the video game arcade in Stranger Things 2 is the Palace Arcade. Which 1980s movie inspired this name?

(21) What type of candy bar does Dustin Henderson feed his Upside Down pet Dart in season two of Stranger Things?

(22) What is the name of the book that Hopper reads to Eleven in the cabin in season two? We also saw Hopper reading this to his late daughter in flashbacks.

(23) What is the favourite candy of Will Byers?

(24) What is Dr Brenner's first name?

(25) Which nostril does Eleven bleed from when she uses her

powers?

(26) The acronym for Hawkins Power and Light, the cover name for the secret government agency meddling with the Upside Down in season one, is HPL. What is HPL a meta reference to?

(27) In which year does Stranger Things 4 take place?

(28) Which 1980s movie inspired Steve and Robin's sailor suits at Scoops Ahoy in Stranger Things 3?

(29) What is the name of the roller rink where Eleven is bullied in Stranger Things 4?

(30) Which character has the most lines in season two of Stranger Things?

(31) Troy is the nasty school bully in season one. What is Troy's full name?

(32) Out of the four main boys in Stranger Things, which character is the only one not to have any siblings?

(33) Max has a Madrid skateboard in Stranger Things 2. Which famous movie character from the 1980s also used this skateboard?

(34) The song 'Should I Stay or Should I Go' features heavily in season one. Which band performed this song?

(35) What is the name of the government agent who shoots dead the diner owner Benny in the first episode of season one?

(36) In which season did Sadie Sink as Max join the show?

(37) Why does Steve keep referring to Marty McFly from Back to the Future as Alex P Keaton in Stranger Things 3?

(38) Who is the captain of the Hawkins High basketball team in Stranger Things 4?

(39) Which short-lived and controversial soft drink do we see characters drinking in Stranger Things 3?

(40) What are the names of Hopper's two police deputies?

(41) What is Jim Hopper's favourite type of beer?

(42) What film is playing at the Hawkins cinema in season one of Stranger Things?

(43) Sean Astin played Bob Newby in Stranger Things 2 but he originally auditioned for another part. Which role did Astin originally audition for?

(44) In the first ever episode (The Vanishing of Will Byers), the diner owner Benny gives Eleven some ice cream. What flavour is the ice cream that Eleven is eating?

(45) What codename do the boys use to refer to their quest to find the missing Will Byers in season one?

(46) The fantastic Halloween heavy trailer for Stranger Things 2 made use of a famous horror themed eighties pop song. What is the name of this song?

(47) How many girls tested for the part of Eleven before Millie Bobby Brown was cast?

(48) Maya Hawke plays Robin in Stranger Things. What is Robin's surname?

(49) What are the names of Mike and Nancy's parents in Stranger Things?

ANSWERS TO QUESTIONS 1-49 ON PAGE 87

(50) Can you name the German electronic music band which heavily influenced the Stranger Things music score?

(51) What is the name of Hopper's secretary at the Hawkins police station?

(52) When the kids are hiding in the school in the season one finale, Dustin is desperate to find the school's supply of which food item?

(53) When we see Mike's plane land in California at the start of the episode Vecna's Curse, which film does this shot pay homage to?

(54) Which one of Mike's Star Wars toys does Eleven levitate in season one of Stranger Things?

(55) Jonathan has a poster for a famous horror film on his wall in season one. What is the name of this film?

(56) Which member of the Stranger Things cast became the youngest person to be appointed as a UNICEF Goodwill Ambassador?

(57) What is the name of the Byers family dog in season one?

(58) What job did Charlie Heaton do before he became an actor?

(59) Where does Bob Newby work in Stranger Things 2?

(60) When they made the first season of Stranger Things, who was the first of the kids to be cast in the show?

(61) In the season two episode The Lost Sister, Eleven travels to a big city to find Kali. What is the name of the city?

(62) Which celebrity endorses Steve Harrington's most beloved hairspray in Stranger Things 2?

(63) What is the name of the arcade game that Dustin plays at the start of Stranger Things 2?

(64) What was the 'Upside Down' called in the original Stranger Things scripts?

(65) What is the name of the password required to enter Will Byers' woodland clubhouse 'Castle Byers'?

(66) Holly Wheeler in Stranger Things is played by twins Anniston and Tinsley Price. What other famous television role did these twins play?

(67) Stranger Things might be set in Indiana but it is not filmed in that state. In which state is Stranger Things actually shot?

(68) In season three, Dustin suggests that the Soviets might be dabbling in Promethium in their underground lair. What is Promethium a pop culture reference to?

(69) Which horror film sequel inspired the hospital logos and uniforms in Stranger Things 3?

(70) In the second season episode Will the Wise, Dr Owens says to Nancy and Jonathan that - "Men of science have made abundant mistakes of every kind." Who is this quote a reference to?

(71) In which season four episode does Eleven not make an appearance?

(72) What is the name of the artist who designs and illustrates the Stranger Things posters?

(73) Kali is a character we meet in season two. She also grew up in the Hawkins lab like Eleven and is known as 'Eight'. What is Kali's special power?

(74) Steve and Nancy have dinner with Barb's parents in season two. What is on the menu?

(75) The Duffer Brothers said they got over a dozen rejections when they tried to pitch Stranger Things to networks. The Duffers said there was one specific thing networks didn't like about the show and wanted them to get rid of. What was that?

(76) Millie Bobby Brown said she did not enjoy eating the fries at Benny's diner while shooting The Vanishing of Will Byers. Why did Millie find these scenes such an ordeal?

(77) What name does Dustin give the hill where he places his radio tower in Stranger Things 3?

(78) What type of car does Billy Hargrove drive in Stranger Things?

(79) Millie Bobby Brown was billed as Millie Brown when she first started acting. Why did she add 'Bobby' to her name?

(80) Out of the four completed seasons, which episode of Stranger Things required the most visual effects?

(81) Out of the four main boys in Stranger Things, who is the oldest in real life?

(82) What is the name of the place where Steve and Robin work in Stranger Things 4?

(83) The kids in the Stranger Things cast started a private group chat when the show began. What name did they give this group?

(84) Which movie actors are Steve and Nancy dressed as at the fancy dress Halloween party in Stranger Things 2?

(85) Can you name the manga series and later anime which the Duffers said was a big influence on the character of

Eleven?

(86) Whereabouts in the Soviet Union is Hopper being held prisoner in Stranger Things 4?

(87) In the finale of Stranger Things 3, Dustin has to sing a duet with Suzie and they belt out an impromptu cover of the catchy theme song to the 1984 fantasy film The Neverending Story. The original theme song was sung by Limahl with Beth Anderson. What is the name of the band that Limahl was the lead singer for?

(88) Which Stephen King story, where a blanket of monster festooned fog descends on a town after a military experiment, was an obvious inspiration on both the Upside Down and the story in Stranger Things?

(89) The Hellfire Club is the name of a secret society in which famous Marvel comic?

(90) In which European country did Stranger Things 4 do some location shooting for the Soviet Union scenes?

(91) Nancy Wheeler has a Debbie Harry calendar in season one. Which band was Debbie Harry was the lead singer of?

(92) Who supplied the birth certificate for Eleven so that Hopper could adopt her at the end of season two?

(93) Which famous video game franchise (later adapted into films) was a huge influence on the look of the Upside Down in Stranger Things?

(94) What is the full name of Dustin's mother in Stranger Things?

(95) What was Dr Brenner called in the pilot script?

(96) What is the name of Dustin's turtle?

(97) What is Eleven's real name?

(98) Which character has the most lines in Stranger Things 3?

(99) In season two, Hopper's secret morse code knock at the cabin to Eleven is (••—/•••). What is the translation of this?

ANSWERS TO QUESTIONS 50-99 ON PAGE 91

(100) The first season of Stranger Things, in terms of its concept, is very reminiscent of a famous 1963 Richard Matheson penned Twilight Zone episode. What is the name of this Twilight Zone episode?

(101) Which members of the Stranger Things cast knew each other before the show?

(102) Who was the last of the kids to be cast in Stranger Things when they made season one?

(103) "It's a trap!" shouts Mike when the Flayer possessed Will sends the soldiers into the tunnels in Stranger Things 2. Which movie character does Mike quote with this line?

(104) In what year was the company Netlix founded?

(105) Which two members of the Stranger Things cast became a couple after meeting on the show?

(106) What is the name of the M. Night Shyamalan television show the Duffer Brothers worked on before Stranger Things?

(107) In what episode is the Snow Ball dance first mentioned?

(108) At the end of season three, Steve and Robin go to the video store to ask for a job. Keith is the manager and asks them to name their three favourite movies. Which three films

does Robin list?

(109) What is Bob Newby's nickname?

(110) In what year did Eleven banish Peter Ballard (aka Henry Creel aka Vecna!) to the Upside Down?

(111) What name does Dustin give his radio tower in season three?

(112) What is the lowest rated episode of Stranger Things on IMBD?

(113) Which Stranger Things cast member is the youngest person ever to feature on the Time 100 list of the 100 most influential people?

(114) The Soviets are the villains in season three. In what year did the Soviet Union collapse and dissolve?

(115) Who composes the Stranger Things music score?

(116) In which season of the show was Erica Sinclair introduced?

(117) What book is Suzie is reading when we finally meet her in the season three finale?

(118) What is the name of the store where Eleven steals the Eggo waffles in season one?

(119) Which movie character inspired Argyle's name?

(120) Which two seasons of Stranger Things had an extra episode?

(121) The nerdy and sarcastic Keith is the Palace Arcade manager in season two and then works at Family Video in season three. What snack food is Keith always eating?

(122) In season four, Eleven has to go to an underground missile silo in the desert to get her powers back. What is the location of this secret base?

(123) What is the name of the episode where Dr Brenner finally dies?

(124) What is the name of the librarian at the Hawkins public library?

(125) What is the name of the real life mall which was used for the Starcourt Mall scenes in Stranger Things 3?

(126) In the episode E Pluribus Unum, who played the younger version of Max in the flashbacks?

(127) What is the name of Eleven's catatonic mother in Stranger Things?

(128) Troy, the school bully in season one, has a sidekick. What is the name of Troy's partner in crime?

(129) Steve Harrington was originally going to be killed off in season one. Is this statement true or false?

(130) In which episode do Mike Wheeler and Eleven meet each other for the first time in Stranger Things?

(131) How does Bob Newby die in Stranger Things?

(132) What is the name of the army officer who is always trying to capture Eleven in Stranger Things 4?

(133) Dustin calls himself 'Gold Leader' on the walkie-talkie in Stranger Things. What famous movie character is this inspired by?

(134) Of the six main 'kids' in Stranger Things, who is the youngest in real life?

(135) When Hopper sneaks into the morgue in season one, he encounters a state trooper. What book is the state trooper reading?

(136) What is the name of the girl that Robin has a crush on in Stranger Things 4?

(137) What is the name of the asylum where Victor Creel is incarcerated in Stranger Things 4?

(138) What arcade game has Max - much to Dustin's annoyance - got a high score on in Stranger Things 2?

(139) The void of nothingness that Eleven enters in Stranger Things for 'remote viewing' was inspired by which film?

(140) What is the real name of the diner which doubled for Benny's Burgers in Stranger Things?

(141) What nationality is Dacre Montgomery?

(142) Steve and Dustin are now an established double act in Stranger Things. What was the name of the episode where these two characters teamed up for the first time?

(143) Which other part in Stranger Things did Joe Keery audition for before he was cast as Steve Harrington?

(144) What film is showing at the Hawkins cinema in Stranger Things 2?

(145) What television show inspired Hopper's tropical shirt in season three?

(146) What other part in the show did Noah Schnapp audition for before he was cast as Will Byers?

(147) Where exactly is Barb when she is attacked by the Demogorgon in Stranger Things?

(149) In the episode The Body, the boys take Eleven to the school to use the ham radio. When they encounter the teacher Mr Clarke they pretend Eleven is their cousin. What country do the boys say Eleven is from?

ANSWERS TO QUESTIONS 100-149 ON PAGE 96

(150) Billy calls a kid "lard ass" at the pool in Stranger Things 3. Which 1980s movie is this a reference to?

(151) How many words does Millie Bobby Brown as Eleven speak in the first season of Stranger Things?

(152) Hawkins and Hopper are both the names of characters in a famous 1980s sci-fi horror action film. Can you name the film?

(153) Robert Englund plays Victor Creel in Stranger Things 4. Which horror movie character is Englund most famous for?

(154) What type of sneakers (trainers) does Dustin Henderson wear in season one?

(155) Bob Newby has a JVC GR-C1 camcorder in Stranger Things 2. What 1980s movie is this camera most associated with?

(156) Which episode in season one did the Duffer Brothers say they liked the most?

(157) How much did it cost the production team to buy Hopper's trailer home in season one?

(158) In season one, Mike Wheeler has a poster for a fantasy film by Jim Henson on his wall. What is the name of this film?

(159) Which horror movie character does Max Mayfield dress

up as for Halloween night in Stranger Things 2?

(160) When Jonathan rents some movies from the video store for Halloween in Stranger Things 2, which three films does he pick?

(161) The many children who auditioned for Stranger Things were required to act some scenes from two 1980s movies. What were the names of these two films?

(162) Dustin's elaborate bequiffed hair at the Snow Ball dance in Stranger Things 2 is a reference to which film?

(163) Which character did the Duffers say was the hardest to cast in Stranger Things?

(164) When Billy threatens to run the Ghostbusters costumed boys over in season two, he asks Max if he'll get more 'points' if he hits them all at once. What film is this a reference to?

(165) What brand of sneakers does Robin wear in season three?

(166) What do main cast regulars Millie Bobby Brown and Charlie Heaton have in common?

(167) What is the music we hear when Eleven opens the music box in the Wheeler house in season one?

(168) Where does Eleven spend most of season one living?

(169) Maya Hawke has famous parents. Can you name them?

(170) The Lost Sister includes some music taken from a deleted a scene in a John Carpenter film. Can you name the film in question?

(171) Francesca Reale plays the lifeguard Heather Holloway in Stranger Things 3. Which other part in the show did Reale

originally audition for?

(172) Where does Argyle work in Stranger Things 4?

(173) What is the name of Nancy's young newspaper colleague who is killed by Vecna in the second episode of Stranger Things 4?

(174) In what episode are Mike and Eleven finally reunited in Stranger Things 2?

(175) Who does Dustin eventually dance with at the Snow Ball after all the mean girls snub him?

(176) To evade the baddies at the mall in Stranger Things 3, Steve, Robin, Dustin, and Erica hide in the cinema. What film is playing in the cinema?

(177) Which two actors in the show were upgraded to full recurring cast members for Stranger Things 2?

(178) Gabriella Pizzolo plays Dustin's girlfriend Suzie in Stranger Things. What does Pizzolo have in common with Gaten Matazarro?

(179) Before she was cast as Erica Sinclair, Priah Ferguson was already a big fan of Stranger Things. Is this statement true or false?

(180) What is the name of the famous horror film which Finn Wolfhard was cast in just prior to Stranger Things?

(181) What country was Millie Bobby Brown born in?

(182) What was unusual about Finn Wolfhard's Stranger Things audition?

(183) Which famous comic book film did Millie Bobby Brown unsuccessfully audition for before she became famous for

Stranger Things?

(184) Millie Bobby Brown is deaf in one ear. Is this statement true or false?

(185) Which fast food beverage does Alexei in Stranger Things 3 have a fondness for?

(186) Where did Max Mayfield move to Hawkins from?

(187) In what season four episode does Eleven finally get her full powers back?

(188) In which city does Suzie live in Stranger Things?

(189) What was unusual about the first teaser for Stranger Things 3?

(190) What weapon does Lucas Sinclair use in the early seasons of Stranger Things?

(191) In what season of the show was Murray Bauman introduced?

(192) When her powers are fully restored in Stranger Things 4, what feat does Eleven perform to confirm this?

(193) What food did the Stranger Things kids hand out to celebrities at the 2016 Emmy awards?

(194) In which season of the show do we not see any of the kids at school?

(195) When Hopper becomes drunk at the restaurant in Stranger Things 3, after Joyce fails to turn up for their date, what is the background music we hear?

(196) Matthew Modine turned down the part of Dr Brenner when it was first offered to him. Is this statement true or false?

(197) What did Sadie Sink have to learn to do when she was cast as Max Mayfield?

(198) At the start of season three, Dustin has returned from summer camp. What is the name of the camp he attended?

(199) Gaten Matarazzo read for the parts of Lucas and Mike before he was cast as Dustin. Is this statement true or false?

ANSWERS TO QUESTIONS 150-199 ON PAGE 100

(200) In the season one episode The Bathtub, Mr Clarke is seen at home with his girlfriend watching a movie. What movie is he watching?

(201) What make of car does Hopper steal at the gas station in Stranger Things 3?

(202) What are the five stages of Demogorgon development?

(203) Season two begins with a car chase prologue involving Kali's gang. In which city does this car chase take place?

(204) In which episode does Mike kiss Eleven for the first time?

(205) In season one, Holly Wheeler is deliberately made to look like a specific movie character. Can you name this character?

(206) In which year did the Demogorgon first appear in Dungeons & Dragons?

(207) In which season of Stranger Things do we see Eleven attending a school for the first time?

(208) What is the first season of the show where Will Byers

appears in every episode?

(209) Which character has the most screen time in Stranger Things 3?

(210) What are the names of the two sitcoms that Paul Reiser is famous for featuring in?

(211) In which episode does Bob Newby die?

(212) Which two actors in the show were upgraded to full cast members for season four?

(213) What subject does Mr Clarke teach at Hawkins Middle School?

(214) What is the common denominator between many of the characters who have died in Stranger Things?

(215) What is the name of the actor who plays Vecna in Stranger Things 4?

(216) What is the name of Max's guidance counsellor in Stranger Things 4?

(217) What is the name of the Arnold Schwarzenegger like Soviet enforcer who makes life so difficult for Hopper in Stranger Things 3?

(218) The special effects team said they found it tricky to make Dustin's pet creature Dart seem cute and endearing. What specific reason did they cite for this?

(219) What is Steve Harrington's weapon of choice?

(220) Which two characters have to go to the depths beneath the Hawkins lab to close the Gate in the season two finale?

(221) Part of Sleepy Hollow Farm in Powder Spring, Georgia,

is used as the exterior for a specific house in Stranger Things. Which house is this?

(222) What is the name of Steve's best friend in season one?

(223) Which dead character makes a brief appearance in the fourth episode of season four?

(224) Which war did Hopper take part in when he was in the military?

(225) What is the first season of the show not to feature an appearance by Mr Clarke?

(226) In what year is season one of Stranger Things set?

(227) Hopper dispatches a Demogorgon with a sword in the season four finale. What film is this sword a reference to?

(228) What is the name of the untrustworthy smuggler that Joyce and Murray have to meet in Stranger Things 4?

(229) What is the name of the book Karen Wheeler is reading by the pool near the start of Stranger Things 3?

(230) What does Noah Schnapp dislike the most about his character Will Byers?

(231) Which Stranger Things cast member competed in the 1996 Paralympics in Atlanta?

(232) Bob Newby asks (jokingly) if there is "treasure" at the end of Will's crayon map in Stranger Things 2. What film is this a reference to?

(233) The scene in season one where Jonathan and Nancy find an injured deer in the woods and it is yanked away from something unseen was inspired by a near identical scene in a survival horror video game. Can you name this game?

(234) What is the name of the lake in season four where Steve finds the underwater portal?

(235) What does Eleven use as a sensory deprivation water tank in the season four finale?

(236) What 1980s police action show does Hopper say Eleven is a fan of in Stranger Things 3?

(237) Hopper has to go Merril's farm to investigate the rotting pumpkin patches in Stranger Things 2. Which two Stephen King stories feature a character named Merril?

(238) What is the name of the Denis Villeneuve film which the Duffers said was a surprisingly big influence on Stranger Things?

(239) In which season two episode do Steve and Nancy break up as a romantic couple?

(240) In the season four episode The Dive, Steve's gang have to meet up with Eddie in the woods. What specific location do they agree to meet at?

(241) The arcade scenes in season two feature several arcade machines in the background or being used by characters. Can you name four of these arcade games?

(242) What is the name of the episode where Dustin's pet Dart gets loose in the school?

(243) Sadie Sink nearly missed out on playing Max because of a specific reason. Can you guess what this was?

(244) What did the building used for the Palace Arcade used to be before it was renovated by the Stranger Things production crew?

(245) What is the name of the mean girl who makes life a

misery at school for Eleven at the start of Stranger Things 4?

(246) What food does Dustin bring for the mission in the woods by the boys to find Will in season one?

(247) What song by The Bangles features in The Weirdo on Maple Street?

(248) What song is playing during the mall montage featuring Eleven and Max in The Mallrats?

(249) When he prepares a Dungeons & Dragons campaign in The Case of the Missing Lifeguard, Will has some music playing. What film is this music from?

ANSWERS TO QUESTIONS 200-249 ON PAGE 103

(250) What sort of sneakers does Dustin wear to the Snow Ball dance in Stranger Things 2?

(251) Which actor does Nancy have a poster of on her bedroom wall in season one?

(252) What was the first scene ever shot for Stranger Things?

(253) What beverage was brought back in 2019 for a short marketing release to coincide with Stranger Things 3?

(254) What do Dustin, Lucas, and Erica use in The Massacre at Hawkins Lab to communicate with their friends trapped in the Upside Down?

(255) What is the occupation of Joyce Byers in Stranger Things 4?

(256) Which character became the main host for the Mind Flayer in season three?

(257) Which food item does Dustin complain about at the funeral of Will Byers in season one?

(258) Why were Nancy and Jonathan fired from the Hawkins post newspaper in season three?

(259) In season three, what snack food does Eleven use her powers to get out of the vending machine for Mike in the hospital?

(260) What is the name of the Russian prison guard who tries to help Hopper escape in season four?

(261) Can you name the two films which were the biggest influence on the Stranger Things title sequence?

(262) What do the sexist men at the Hawkins Post call Nancy in season three?

(263) What was the character of Kali originally going to be called?

(264) What is the season one episode title The Flea and the Acrobat a reference to?

(265) Peter Gabriel's cover version of Heroes features in Stranger Things at various points in various seasons. Who originally sang this song?

(266) Who are the four members of the Stranger Things 3 gang known as the Scoop Troop?

(267) In which film did Winona Ryder make her movie debut?

(268) There is a big technology anachronism in the Palace Arcade scenes in Stranger Things 2. Can you name the anachronism?

(269) How does Dr Brenner die in Stranger Things?

(270) Danish actress Linnea Berthelsen plays Kali in Stranger Things. Where was Linnea Berthelsen born?

(271) What was the episode budget on Stranger Things 4?

(272) Which actress does Dustin say his girlfriend Suzie is 'hotter' than in season three?

(273) In season one, what does Hopper tell his secretary mornings are for?

(274) What is the name of the Henderson family cat in season two?

(275) Who, according to Hopper in season one, had a bird land on her head because the bird thought her hair was a nest?

(276) What does Will cough up in the bathroom at the end of season one?

(277) What mask does Eddie borrow off Max in season four to hide his face in the trailer park?

(278) Why can't Eleven get to Hawkins to battle Vecna in the season four finale?

(279) How did Eleven escape from the Upside Down after the events of season one?

(280) Who does Robin tell Steve in season three she had a crush on when they were at school?

(281) What job was Joe Keery doing when he learned he'd been cast as Steve Harrington in Stranger Things?

(282) What is the drawing on the Byers fridge in season three?

(283) What is the name of the director of the mental asylum that Nancy and Robin visit in Stranger Things 4?

(284) What grisly thing happens to the victims of Vecna as they die?

(285) What is the most prized possession of Eddie Munson?

(286) After Nancy shoots Vecna in the season four finale, they find no trace of his body outside where he fell. What movie scene is this a homage to?

(287) What television show did Shannon Purser join after she left Stranger Things?

(288) What did Dacre Montgomery suffer from shooting the lifeguard scenes in Stranger Things 3?

(289) What part-time job did Shannon Purser have when she was cast as Barb?

(290) What is the name of the character that Paul Reiser played in Aliens?

(291) How long did it take to shoot the Snow Ball dance scenes in the season two finale?

(292) What is the name of the song we hear when Will Byers is being given the kiss of life in the season one finale?

(293) In season two, Hopper hides Eleven at his cabin in the woods. Who did the cabin originally belong to?

(294) In the season one finale, who ventures into the Upside Down to rescue Will Byers?

(295) In what American state was Sadie Sink born?

(296) In a flashback in the first ever episode, Joyce visits Will in the woods and surprises him with tickets to a screening of a film. Which film does she have tickets to see?

(297) What was the inspiration for Hopper's police jeep and uniform?

(298) Cary Elwes, who plays Mayor Kline in Stranger Things 3, is most famous for which 1980s movie?

(299) In what film did Natalia Dyer make her movie debut?

ANSWERS TO QUESTIONS 250-299 ON PAGE 107

(300) What type of camera does Jonathan Byers own in season one?

(301) What type of car does Joyce Byers drive in season one?

(302) At the end of season three, Steve bumps into a cardboard standee in the video store. What is the name of the actress depicted on the standee?

(303) What is the name of the medical condition Gaten Matarazzo has suffered from and spoken about?

(304) Maya Hawke as Robin says the line in "I'll take those odds" in Stranger Things 3. What film does this line come from?

(305) What is the name of the estranged former husband of Joyce Byers?

(306) What do Jonathan and Nancy have for breakfast when they stay at Murray Bauman's house in season two?

(307) Which 1980 Stephen King novel, later turned into a 1984 film, was a very obvious influence on Eleven and the lab scenes in Stranger Things?

(308) In season one of Stranger Things, the school bully Troy calls Mike's gang 'losers'. What is this a reference to?

(309) What type of sneakers does Mike Wheeler wear in season one?

(310) What is the name of the episode where Eleven saves Mike and Dustin from the school bullies at the quarry?

(311) Characters use Polaroid cameras in Stranger Things 2. What was novel about Polaroid cameras in the 1980s?

(312) When the boys discuss their Dungeons & Dragons campaign at the end of season one of Stranger Things and lament the fact that it wasn't longer, what is the subtext of this dialogue?

(313) What was the first ever scene in Stranger Things?

(314) What two comic books do Max and Eleven peruse in Max's bedroom in season three?

(315) Which character has the last line of dialogue in Stranger Things 4?

(316) In which season of the show does the character of Jim Hopper have the least amount of lines?

(317) What holiday does season four take place around?

(318) What does Hopper go to the woods to do at the end of season one?

(319) What was Lucas Sinclair called in the pilot script?

(320) What horror television show was the Wheeler house interior set also used in?

(321) What was the original concept for the character of Mr Clarke in the pitch document?

(322) What is the name of the episode where Steve and

Jonathan have a fight in the alley?

(323) During the cabin siege in The Mind Flayer, what does Mike Wheeler pick up to use as a potential weapon?

(324) In what season of the show do Hopper and Eleven end up with the same haircut?

(325) Which one of the characters in Stranger Things did the Duffer Brothers say they related to the most?

(326) In which season of the show does Eleven have the most lines?

(327) What is the name of the season three episode where Eleven tells Mike "I dump your ass"?

(328) In which episode do we see for the first time that Eleven is secretly living with Hopper and he has become a surrogate father to her?

(329) What is the name of the area where the kids go trick or treating in Stranger Things 2?

(330) Whose idea was it for Mike and Eleven to kiss at the Snow Ball dance?

(331) Who does the arcade manager Keith want a date with in Stranger Things 2?

(332) We see in season three that Max has a crush on a famous actor. Can you name this actor?

(333) In what year did Stranger Things first become available to stream?

(334) Why Does Dustin telephone Mr Clarke at home in season one?

(335) Eleven's curly hair in season two is Millie Bobby Brown's natural hair. True or false?

(336) What is the full name of Troy's sidekick bully?

(337) Dustin names one of the groups in Stranger Things 3 the Griswold family. What film is this a reference to?

(338) How does Jason Carver die in season four?

(339) Who is the first to dive into the lake after Steve in season four when it becomes apparent he might be in trouble?

(340) Finn Wolfhard has been in two music bands. Can you name them?

(341) How did Millie Bobby Brown teach herself to do an American accent?

(342) What is the highest rated episode of Stranger Things on IMDB?

(343) What is the highest rated Stranger Things season finale on IMDB?

(344) Eleven pointing to the picture of the missing Will in season one is a nod to a scene in which 1985 film?

(345) How much weight did David Harbour lose before Stranger Things 4?

(346) Which episode in season one did Millie Bobby Brown say she liked the best?

(347) What Twilight Zone episode is the title The Weirdo on Maple Street an allusion to?

(348) Which stunt in season one did Netflix insist had to feature in the trailer for the show?

(349) Why does Mike get sad and reflective when he picks up a dinosaur toy early in season two?

ANSWERS TO QUESTIONS 300-349 ON PAGE 111

(350) Which large object does Eleven use her powers to try and move in The Lost Sister?

(351) Who does Billy Hargrove flirt with in The Gate when he's out trying to find Max?

(352) What is the name of the James Bond film that David Harbour appeared in?

(353) What is the name of the actor who plays Mike and Nancy's father?

(354) What is Bob's death in Stranger Things 2 a homage to?

(355) Which member of the Stranger Things cast has a twin sister?

(356) What is the name of the Hawkins Tigers basketball player killed by Vecna in the lake in season four?

(357) What is the name of the actress who plays Mike and Nancy's mother?

(358) Which episode did Finn Wolfhard say was his favourite in season two?

(359) How old was Millie Bobby Brown when she played Eleven in season one?

(360) Max drives a car in Stranger Things 2 but is too small to reach the pedals. What movie is this a reference to?

(361) What type of watch does Mike have in season one?

(362) What is the first season of the show where Nancy and Jonathan hardly spend any time together?

(363) What is the name of the Soviet doctor who tortures Steve in season three?

(364) Who did Finn Wolfhard say he found scarier - Pennywise the Clown or the Demogorgon?

(365) Why do Dr Brenner and Dr Owens eventually fall out with one another in season four?

(366) Which singer acts as a talisman to Max in season four?

(367) Which type of insect was Henry Creel especially fond of?

(368) In which season one episode does Steve smash Jonathan's camera?

(369) Eleven impersonates ("People are going to be agahst!") an actress while watching television alone in the cabin in season two. What is the name of the television show she is watching?

(370) What is the name of Mr Clarke's girlfriend in season one?

(371) What are Mike and Eleven in Stranger Things known as by fans because of their romance?

(372) What is the name of the little girl seen crying at Will's funeral in season one?

(373) When Steve is taken by surprise by DeomoDogs at the junkyard in season two, which movie scene is this a homage to?

(374) What does 'mouthbreather' mean?

(375) Who played the school bully Troy in season one?

(376) Why does Dustin have to sing The Neverending Story song for Suzie in the season three finale?

(377) What does 'Pollywog' mean?

(378) What song is Mr Clarke listening to when he is visited by Joyce in season three?

(379) Which real company was the main inspiration for the fictional Scoops Ahoy?

(380) Who did Sean Astin play in Peter Jackson's Lord of the Rings trilogy?

(381) What was the split between practical and digital effects in season one of Stranger Things?

(382) In what season of the show do Eleven and Max become friends?

(383) In what year was the first sensory deprivation tank (or chamber) invented?

(384) Which character have Winona Ryder and Maya Hawke both played away from Stranger Things?

(385) Which popular long running children's show did a Stranger Things parody in 2017?

(386) Who did Mark Steger play in season one of Stranger Things?

(387) We first see the parents of Lucas Sinclair in season two. Is this statement true or false?

(388) Shawn Levy is a producer and director on Stranger Things. In which episode does he have a cameo?

(389) What is the name of the film which supposedly inspired Kali's gang in Stranger Things 2?

(390) Which character has the most lines in Stranger Things 4?

(391) Which character has the first line spoken in Stranger Things 4?

(392) What is Mayor Larry Kline's wife called?

(393) The first teaser trailer for Stranger Things 2 used a real 80s Eggo commercial featuring child actor Jason Hervey. Can you name the famous television show that Hervey later appeared in?

(394) In season one, what does Eleven do to the bully Troy at Will's school memorial?

(395) What is the name of The X-Files episode which is often alleged to have been an influence on Stranger Things?

(396) What were Eggo waffles called when they first appeared in supermarkets?

(397) In season one, O'Bannon is the name of the state trooper who was part of the conspiracy to stop Will's 'body' from being examined. What is the name O'Bannon a reference to?

(398) Which 1980 Ken Russell film was an important influence on Stranger Things?

(399) We learn that Murray has been taking classes in something in Stranger Things 4. What has he been taking classes in?

(400) At the Palace Arcade in Stranger Things 2 you can see an arcade game called Quest for the Space Knife. Is this a real game or a fake game?

(401) What is the name of the song that plays during Will's funeral in season one?

(402) We see a Peterbilt truck in the season two episode Dig Dug. What is this a reference to?

(403) What does Mike do to his scrambled eggs in season one that so disgusts Nancy?

(404) In order to escape from Vecna in season four, Max tries to go to a happy place in her memories. What 'happy place' from season two does she end up?

(405) In which season does Dustin take his first trip into the Upside Down?

(406) How many Instagram followers did Millie Bobby Brown have before Stranger Things came out?

(407) When Joyce fails to turn up to her dinner date with Hopper in Stranger Things 3, a drunken Hopper says "I can do anything I want. I'm the chief of police." What film is this line taken from?

(408) Where was Noah Schnapp when he learned he'd been cast in Stranger Things?

(409) Eleven has a scar on her shin in Stranger Things 4. Where did this scar come from?

(410) The boys use TRC-214 walkie-talkies in Stranger things.

What radius did these walkie-talkies have in real life?

(411) Which 1939 film does Suzie have a poster for in her room in season three?

(412) In the episode titled The Case Of The Missing Lifeguard, Steve and Dustin follow a pony tailed man because they believe he is an 'evil' Russian. He turns out though to be an aerobics instructor conducting a Jazzercise class. What song does the instructor play on his stereo for his class?

(413) Hopper wears a wristband in season one. In later seasons Eleven wears this wristband. Where does this wristband come from?

(414) What does Will Byers give to Erica at the end of season three?

(415) The Goonies is one of the films playing at the Starcourt Mall cinema. Is this statement true or false?

(416) In which season four episode does Mike first go to California to visit Eleven?

(417) Which member of the Stranger Things cast commuted from New York to shoot his scenes in season one?

(418) How many episodes does Paul Reiser as Dr Sam Owens appear in during season three?

(419) When he escapes from the prison in the episode Dear Billy, what food does Hopper find a stash of?

(420) What country did Victor Creel have to go and fight in during World War 2?

(421) What type of car does Steve Harrington drive?

(422) What does the term 'ham' radio mean?

(423) What does Eddie Munson have tattooed on the bottom of his right arm?

(424) In the original pitch booklet designed to sell Stranger Things, in what year did the show take place?

(425) How did the original pitch booklet for Stranger Things describe Mike and Eleven?

(426) How did Hopper's daughter die in the original pitch booklet for Stranger Things?

(427) Why does Hopper think he might be to blame for his daughter's illness and death?

(428) When Eleven enters the void in Stranger Things 3 and struggles through gusting wind with a red stormy sky and dark clouds all around her, what is this a homage to?

(429) What comical prosthetic effects mishap befell Dacre Montgomery during the production of season three?

(430) Which two Stranger Things cast members have used the same stunt double?

(431) What is the name of the Wes Craven film which the Duffer Brothers say kickstarted their love of horror?

(432) In which American state was Caleb McLaughlin born?

(433) What was Benny's Burgers in the pilot script?

(434) What did David Harbour say was the worst thing about wearing the Hazmat suit for the season one finale?

(435) How old is Eleven supposed to be in season one?

(436) Which one of the Stranger Things kids plays a character older than his real life age?

(437) During the 'last supper' the prisoners have in the season four episode The Dive, what does Hopper take from the feast?

(438) In season four, who do the unsuspecting locals think is responsible for the murders in Hawkins?

(439) Why is Lucas drifting apart from Dustin and Mike at the start of Stranger Things 4?

(440) According to Netflix research, how many episodes of Stranger Things does it take to get a viewer hooked and in binge mode?

(441) What is the name of the famous stage musical Gaten Matarazzo appeared in when he was eleven?

(442) When Stranger Things 2 was released, on which show did Millie Bobby Brown perform a Stranger Things season one recap rap?

(443) Who came up with Eleven's flick of the head to indicate she'd violently snapped someone's neck or arm?

(444) Who did Stranger Things fans create a shrine to at the 2017 Comic Con?

(445) Why does Eleven get annoyed with Hopper in Trick or Treat, Freak?

(446) Which season two storyline did the Duffer brothers say they were wary of doing but went ahead with anyway?

(447) When Billy is lifting weights in The Spy, there is a music video on television. Can you name the music video?

(448) What illustration does Will Byers paint in season four?

(449) Why does Bob Newby volunteer to go on the mission to restore the power and security in the Hawkins lab in season

two?

ANSWERS TO QUESTIONS 400-449 ON PAGE 118

(450) Which famous 1980s movie also has characters named Mike and Steve?

(451) In the first episode of the show, Mike's dad is trying to tune the television in. What show is he trying to watch?

(452) Near the end of season two, Dr Owens offers Hopper half of his sandwich in the diner. What movie is this a reference to?

(453) What is the full name of Dustin's girlfriend Suzie?

(454) Which famous movie home is Suzie's house in season four made to resemble?

(455) How does Eddie describe basketball in The Hellfire Club?

(456) In which season does Eleven wear a ring?

(457) Who is Mrs Wheeler's hair in season four inspired by?

(458) Why is Eleven annoyed by Mike's letters in Stranger Things 4?

(459) In season one, we see flashbacks of Eleven undertaking remote viewing sensory deprivation missions. These are supposedly to spy on the Soviet Union but what does Eleven come to suspect in season four was the true purpose of these missions?

(460) Millie Bobby Brown hates Eggo waffles in real life. True or false?

(461) Which character in Stranger Things 4 is fond of the eighties band Musical Youth?

(462) Eleven's longest line in season one is only seven words long. True or false?

(463) Why does Suzie's father confiscate her computer in season four?

(464) Which episode did Shawn Levy say was, in hindsight, probably a mistake to do?

(465) How many season two episodes does Kali appear in?

(466) Stranger Things was the first professional acting job of Shannon Purser. True or false?

(467) Which member of the cast hated Stranger Things being chosen as the show's title and asked the Duffers to change it?

(468) Which season of Stranger Things has a funfair?

(469) Why does Hopper take Joyce to the Hawkins lab in season three?

(470) Who tells Steve in season four that Nancy still loves him?

(471) What does Benny give Eleven to eat in the first episode besides ice cream?

(472) In Stranger Things 2, Hopper makes Eleven a 'Triple-Decker Eggo Extravaganza'. How many calories does Hopper jokingly say this dish has?

(473) When Will walks out of his front door to encounter the shadow monster in MADMAX, what film is this a homage to?

(474) The downtown store Joyce works at in season three

hardly has any customers. Why is this?

(475) What does a parched Hopper drink at the gas station in season three?

(476) What is the name of the John Carpenter film Mike has a poster for in his basement den in season one?

(477) In which season one episode do Eleven and Lucas, who thus far haven't got on very well, become friends and apologise to one another?

(478) Dustin can supposedly bend his body like 'Gumby' when he proposes crawling into the air ducts in season three. Who is Gumby?

(479) How many episodes in a season of Stranger Things does Shawn Levy traditionally direct?

(480) The music that plays while Murray Bauman searches Alexei in Stranger Things 3 is Sid Phillips's Boogie Man. What video game did this music feature on?

(481) Why is Eleven wearing a hoodie in the hospital at the end of season four?

(482) In season four, Argyle suggests that Hopper's cabin is not exactly a Fortress of Solitude to hide Supergirl (Eleven). What is Fortress of Solitude a reference to?

(483) The grandly operatic music we hear during Ballard's origin revelation in The Massacre at Hawkins Lab previously featured in two films. Can you name them?

(484) What did the boys in the cast say they got fed up wearing in Stranger Things 3?

(485) Eleven and Max finding Billy's blood flecked bathroom in Stranger Things 3 is a homage to which film?

(486) Joe Keery loved his Scoops Ahoy costume. Is this true or false?

(487) What happens in the prologue to the opening episode of season three?

(488) In the episode The Dive, Steve ends up in the Upside Down shirtless with brown muddied trousers. What film character does he deliberately resemble here?

(489) Which character in Stranger Things got an officially licensed Halloween mask in 2022?

(490) Which season three episode did Sadie Sink say she found the most exhausting to shoot?

(491) When the crow startles Hopper in the pumpkin field in Stranger Things 2 you hear a music cue from a famous film. What film is this?

(492) Which member of the cast has to cry for real in Stranger Things because they are allergic to the chemical that is commonly used to make actors tear-up?

(493) Which natural phenomenon in nature inspired the Mind Flayer cloud monster in season two?

(494) Why does Mike Wheeler take money from Nancy's room at the start of season two?

(495) In Dungeons & Dragons, which monsters are known as illithids?

(496) Which character in Stranger Things shares a name with a Hindu goddess?

(497) Nimród Antal directed two episodes in season four. What horror sci-fi franchise movie is Nimród Antal most famous for directing?

(498) Millie Bobby Brown found it genuinely scary to do scenes with Vecna in season four. True or false?

(499) The Duffers apparently have a concept for a Stranger Things spin-off show. They said that only one member of the cast correctly deduced what this concept is. Who was that shrewd cast member?

ANSWERS TO QUESTIONS 450-499 ON PAGE 121

(500) On which season two sequence did Joe Keery injure his back?

(501) What does Eleven do to the bully Troy at the quarry in season one?

(502) What does Steve buy Jonathan at the end of season one?

(503) The episode The Body takes its title from a Stephen King story. What was the film adaptation of The Body called?

(504) For which season did David Harbour deliberately put on weight because he wanted Hopper to be more slobbish than ever?

(505) In season one, how does Steve Harrington make amends at the cinema?

(506) Who was Millie Bobby Brown shown a picture of before season one to show what her hair would look like when it was shaved?

(507) Susan Shalhoub Larkin plays Hopper's secretary at the police station. Which actor is Susan Shalhoub Larkin the sister of?

(508) Where was the reunion between Mike and Eleven in

season two originally going to take place?

(509) When Millie Bobby Brown was in the lab sensory deprivation water tank in season one, how did the Duffer Brothers communicate with her?

(510) Who seems to be fond of Saucony sneakers in Stranger Things?

(511) The Hawkins cinema location in season one is at 2 N. Oak St. What is this building in real life?

(512) Who did Noah Schnapp supply the voice to in The Peanuts Movie?

(513) What was mostly used for the meat that Steve and Dustin leave on the railway tracks to attract Dart in season two?

(514) The 1984 comedy film Bachelor Party features in the video store at the end of season three. In what way does this film qualify as a Stranger Things in-joke?

(515) What had to be imported to the shooting locations for the last episode of season one?

(516) Which member of the cast wasn't allowed to say if they would be in season two in order to create some ambiguity concerning the fate of their character?

(517) Who is Steve's red bandana in the tunnels for Stranger Things 2 a tribute to?

(518) Which actor in the cast said he didn't enjoy riding his bike in season one?

(519) Who blasts Vecna with a shotgun in the season four finale?

(520) Which dead character made a brief flashback appearance in season three?

(521) What do Steve's gang throw at Vecna in the season four finale?

(522) Which four characters make up the California road trip gang in season four?

(523) Which character has some Sweet Valley High books in their bedroom in season three?

(524) How does Hopper keep the Demogorgon at bay in The Massacre at Hawkins Lab?

(525) The Duffers say that in preparation for Stranger Things 2 they watched their favourite movie sequels for inspiration. Can you name three films they listed as their favourite sequels?

(526) Who was the 'American' in the Soviet prison at the end of season three?

(527) What dark prank did the Duffers play on Noah Schnapp's mother during the production of season one?

(528) How many calories are there in an Eggo waffle?

(529) In the season three finale, Dustin and Suzy perform the theme song to the 1984 fantasy film The Neverending Story. What song were they originally going to sing?

(530) What is the name of the Cyndi Lauper song which plays during the Snow Ball dance in season two?

(531) What did Millie Bobby Brown say her favourite flavour of Eggo waffles were?

(532) Who is Dustin's mother supporting in the 1984 election?

(533) How old is Holly Wheeler supposed to be in season one?

(534) In which season one scene do we hear Fields of Coral from the 1996 album Oceanic by Vangelis?

(535) When asked which one character she would choose to save in season one, who did Millie Bobby Brown pick?

(536) Joe Keery's girlfriend is Maika Monroe. In which cult 2014 horror film did Maika Monroe play the lead character?

(537) What was the tagline for the first Stranger Things 4 teaser?

(538) Whose creative idea was it for Hopper to sacrifice himself at the end of season three?

(539) What did Barb do to make the Demogorgon notice her?

(540) How does Hopper deduce early in season one that the Hawkins lab have shown him bogus surveillance tapes?

(541) What word in season one does Eleven have no awareness of?

(542) In which season one episode does Dr Brenner visit the Wheeler house?

(543) Finn Wolfhard's Stranger Things audition tape was out of focus. Is this true or false?

(544) At the Halloween party attended by Steve and Nancy in Stranger Things 2, a number of movies are referenced through the costumes. Can you name three of them?

(545) Why did David Harbour want Hopper to have a hat in Stranger Things?

(546) What was 'Justice for Barb'?

(547) In which American state was Natalia Dyer born?

(548) In which season does Mr Clarke have the most lines?

(549) Which cast member worried about a lack of promotion for season one?

ANSWERS TO QUESTIONS 500-549 ON PAGE 125

(550) What did the Duffers say was the first idea they came up with in season two?

(551) Bob Newby suggests to Joyce they should move to Maine in season two. What is this a meta reference to?

(552) Eleven uses television static to enter the void in season two. What film is this a reference to?

(553) When the boys and Eleven bump into Mr Clarke in the school in season one where does Eleven tell him she came from?

(554) What type of car does Jonathan drive?

(555) What military craft does Eleven destroy in season four?

(556) What is the name of the superhero film that Charlie Heaton was in?

(557) What is Dustin dressed as for the Upside Down mission in season four?

(558) Which comedy film sequel does Will Byers say is "supposed to suck" in season four?

(559) Who is used as bait for Vecna in the season four finale?

(560) What year was Eddie Munson originally supposed to graduate?

(561) What is the name of Dr Owens' chief assistant in season four?

(562) Who was the first of the adult cast members to sign up for Stranger Things?

(563) Which Stranger Things characters featured in a Dead By Daylight crossover?

(564) What does Eleven call Hopper's haircut in season four?

(565) What did the children in the cast have to be assigned on the set in the early seasons?

(566) What term does Dustin use on the walkie-talkie for an emergency?

(567) Which cast member in the show said he has always played Dungeons & Dragons?

(568) What did Millie Bobby Brown say she ate before kissing Finn Wolfhard in the season two finale?

(569) After she completed her scenes on season one, what did Shannon Purser want to take home but couldn't manage to get hold of?

(570) What do the two agents assigned to protect the Byers house in season four watch on television?

(571) What is the name of the Madonna song which features in The Case of the Missing Lifeguard?

(572) Which character wears a Timex Weekender watch in season one?

(573) Which member of the Stranger Things cast used to be in a skateboarding team?

(574) Which two members of the cast say they have stolen socks from the costume department?

(575) Dustin has dinner at the Wheeler house in season one. What are they eating?

(576) Who got more screen time in season two than was originally intended because they made the Duffers laugh?

(577) Which cast member said he'd endured about a hundred failed auditions before Stranger Things?

(578) What is the name of the Superman actor who was in a film with Millie Bobby Brown?

(579) Glennellen Anderson plays Nicole in season one. Which other part did she audition for?

(580) What was the art of Polish painter Zdzislaw Beksinski an influence on in Stranger Things?

(581) Charlie Heaton was a huge horror fan - even before Stranger Things. Is this statement true or false?

(582) What did the cast and crew notice flying over the set when they began shooting season two?

(583) What game in the Palace Arcade set did the Duffer Brothers say they played the most between takes?

(584) Who did Andrey Ivchenko play in Stranger Things?

(585) Which season one episode does not feature the Demogorgon?

(586) Which cast member says he always gets a haircut as

soon as shooting is over on a season of Stranger Things?

(587) Lookalikes for which character were hired by Netflix to promote season two at Comic Con?

(588) Which cast member has hosted a Netflix prank show?

(589) In season one, who has the most lines in any one single episode?

(590) What scene did Joseph Quinn have to do for his Eddie Munson audition?

(591) What is the name of the 2014 thriller film the Stranger Things music composers scored? It was this film that put them on the radar of the Duffer Brothers.

(592) Hopper's hat is based on one a famous general and politician used to wear. Can you name the person in question?

(593) Which character in the show did the Duffer Brothers describe as being like the 1980s version of Wikipedia?

(594) How many agents does Eleven take out in Benny's kitchen in the first ever episode?

(595) Who gives Eleven the name 'El'?

(596) Does Mike Wheeler like pineapple on his pizza?

(597) In which season one episode does Hopper find out that Will's body in the morgue is actually a dummy?

(598) How does Eleven throw the boys off the trail of the Hawkins lab in The Flea and the Acrobat?

(599) What are Mike's parting words to his mother before the bike chase in The Bathtub?

ANSWERS TO QUESTIONS 550-599 ON PAGE 128

(600) Why does Dr Owens refuse to burn the tunnels in season two?

(601) Which character in season four mentions the internet?

(602) What set did NASA's Space Environment Simulation Lab inspire in Stranger Things?

(603) When Eleven searches under the floorboards of Hopper's cabin in season two, what does she find?

(604) Who is the character 'Funshine' in Stranger Things?

(605) Why does Eleven's mother only say the words "Breathe. Sunflower. Rainbow. Three to the right. Four to the left. 450."?

(606) Nancy and Jonathan buy traps and weapons in an army surplus store in season one. What does Nancy say when she is asked why they are buying all this stuff?

(607) Does Eleven like pineapple on her pizza?

(608) The moment where Lucas shoots the Demogorgon in the season one finale with his wrist-rocket and it is thrown back (we quickly deduce that Eleven REALLY did this - not Lucas) is a riff on a scene in which film?

(609) What is the name of the Quentin Tarantino film that Maya Hawke appeared in?

(610) Which character in Stranger Things always wears a suit and tie?

(611) What does Joyce hang up in season one in the belief that Will might be able to use them to make contact?

(612) Which cast member has a clown phobia?

(613) What is the (very nerdy) Ghostbusters goof in season two?

(614) What was Gaten Matarazzo banned from doing during the production of season two?

(615) Which cast member said it was a bit surreal to think there was now an action figure bearing his likeness?

(616) Which film was a huge influence on the sound design regarding the clicking noise which heralds the proximity of the Demogorgon?

(617) What is the first episode where the term 'Upside Down' starts to be used?

(618) What is the first episode where we see inside the Upside Down?

(619) What was the first episode of Stranger Things to take place on the same day?

(620) Who brings Joyce a casserole in season one?

(621) Which former member of the Stranger things cast served in the Red Army in real life?

(622) Which two characters near the end of season three wear the same outfits as Eric and Donna from 'That 70s Show?

(623) What vehicle does Hopper deploy in his first failed prison escape attempt in season four?

(624) Who did Dacre Montgomery play in the Power Rangers movie?

(625) When she did her auditions for Stranger Things, Millie

Bobby Brown had no idea that Eleven was going to have superpowers. Is this true or false?

(626) What is the Planck constant?

(627) What season of Stranger Things opens with a paperboy?

(628) What did the kids in Stranger Things like to do the most to bond on the early seasons?

(629) What don't friends do according to Eleven?

(630) In The Spy, Andrew Stanton set up a shot of Joyce walking into a conference room to mimic a similar shot in a 1976 satirical drama film. Can you name this film?

(631) In which season do we see an Ewok cartoon on television?

(632) After completing season three, what did Dacre Montgomery take from the set as a momento of his time on the show?

(633) What did Finn Wolfhard say his favourite scene in season three was?

(634) What magazine does Will Byers have copies of at Castle Byers in season three?

(635) Who has a car phone in season three?

(636) Can you name three films that are promoted or shown at the mall cinema in season three?

(637) Hopper threatens to cut Mayor Kline's finger off with a cigar cutter in Stranger Things 3. What film is this a reference to?

(638) Linnea Berthelsen (as Kali) has more lines in The Lost

Sister than any other character in Stranger Things 2 has in any single one episode. Is this true or false?

(639) In a season two flashback, Eleven wears a red hunting hat in the woods. What famous novel is this hat a reference to?

(640) Joyce driving Will to the lab in season two is shown overhead. What is this a homage to?

(641) What job did Jonathan Byers have in the early plans for Stranger Things?

(642) What fictional realm do the kids liken the Upside Down to in season one?

(643) Which cast member in Stranger Things played Annie on the stage?

(644) What is the name of the smash hit 1984 comedy action movie that Paul Reiser appeared in?

(645) What is the name of Billy Hargrove's stern father?

(646) What was the name of the BBC America series that Millie Bobby Brown starred in before Stranger Things?

(647) Which villain from Harry Potter did the Duffers say was an influence on the Mind Flayer?

(648) Dungeons & Dragons spawned a popular kids cartoon of the same name in 1983. In which season of Stranger Things do we hear some music from this cartoon?

(649) Which character comes up with the term 'DemoDogs'?

ANSWERS TO QUESTIONS 600-649 ON PAGE 131

(650) Our introduction to Dr Owens in season two is a homage to which film?

(651) What comedy show is Brett Gelman also known for?

(652) Which singing star does Bob Newby profess a fondness for in season two?

(653) Why were the bikes ridden by the boys in season one constructed from various different bikes?

(654) How does Bob Newby (tragically) alert the DemoDogs to his presence at the lab in season two?

(655) What does Murray Bauman think is going on in Hawkins when we meet him in season two?

(656) How did Barb cut her hand in The Weirdo on Maple Street?

(657) The scene where the kids push Dustin's radio tower aloft in Suzie, Do You Copy? mimics a famous photograph. Which photograph is this?

(658) What comic book movie featuring David Harbour bombed?

(659) In Stranger Things 2, Joyce asks Will if he remembers the 120-crayon box she bought him when he was eight. Why is this a chronological goof?

(660) Which of the boys in season one was allowed to improvise some of his dialogue?

(661) Which Stranger Things 3 actor has a father who is a renowned heart surgeon in Ukraine?

(662) How long did it take to shoot the final fight featuring Hopper in the finale of Stranger Things 3?

(663) What did Millie Bobby Brown say scared her the most out of ghosts and the Demogorgon?

(664) Is there official product placement in Stranger Things?

(665) What is in the TV dinner that Hopper and Eleven sit down to at the end of the first episode of Stranger Things 2?

(666) Who had a mishap shooting season two when he got stuck in a chair?

(667) Why does Karen decide not to secretly meet Billy in season three?

(668) Who does Hopper find injured on the lab stairs in the season two finale?

(669) Which cast member did a campaign for Yves Saint Laurent?

(670) What type of car are the girls admiring Billy's posterior at the start of Stranger Things 2 sitting against?

(671) What is the most 'neon' season of Stranger Things?

(672) What did Dacre Montgomery say he drew on to play Billy Hargrove in Stranger Things?

(673) What watch was Mike Wheeler supposed to wear in season one?

(674) What song does Hopper, much to the bewilderment of Eleven, dance to at the cabin in season two?

(675) Which character had 199 less lines in season two than in season one?

(676) What natural predator is the Demogorgon likened to in season one?

(677) Where was Shannon Purser when she got a message saying she had been cast in Stranger Things?

(678) Which season two death scene was toned down somewhat to make it less gruesome?

(679) What season one stunt destroyed an expensive camera?

(680) Who had to binge the show when they were cast in Stranger Things 2 because they'd never watched it before?

(681) Which character in Star Wars did Millie Bobby Brown say she would love to play?

(682) In which cult novel is the main character named Nancy Wheeler?

(683) What did the makeup department use to give Will Byers a murky looking tongue in season two?

(684) Which character in season two eats dessert before dinner?

(685) In which season four episode do Jonathan, Will, Mike, and Argyle not appear?

(686) Who grabs the microphone and takes over the town hall meeting in the season four episode The Dive?

(687) Why does Max live in a trailer park in season four?

(688) Who do Mike and Dustin recruit in The Hellfire Club to replace Lucas in the D&D game?

(689) Which season one item does Steve find in the season two finale?

(690) Which cast member's brother had a cameo in season four?

(691) Which member of the cast had to wear front hair extensions in season one because he singed his hair on a candle in the bath?

(692) Which film were the toddlers on the set of season one told the Demogorgon was from so they wouldn't be afraid of it?

(693) Which character's bike in season one is made up of two different colours as if he started painting it but then couldn't be bothered to finish?

(694) Which two characters have a fight in the season two finale?

(695) When Kali and Eleven target Ray Carroll, the lab worker who mistreated Eleven's mother Terry Ives, in season two, what TV show is Carroll watching?

(696) Will tells Mike in season two that the Upside Down visions are like being caught between View-Master slides. What is a View-Master?

(697) Finn Wolfhard, when Mike sees Dustin's hair at the Snow Ball, has an identical line that he says in the movie version of Stephen King's It. What is the line?

(698) What is the name of the 1990s film that Paul Reiser and Matthew Modine were both in?

(699) When Dustin prepares to confront Dart in the cellar in season two, what sports equipment does he put on?

ANSWERS TO QUESTIONS 650-699 ON PAGE 134

(700) What type of vans do the Hawkins lab use?

(701) Why was the scene where the kids hide in the bus in the junkyard in season one something of an ordeal to shoot?

(702) Which two cast members tried to persuade the Duffers not to kill Bob Newby?

(703) What is the name Jonathan Byers commonly assumed to be a reference to?

(704) What type of car does Barb drive?

(705) When she signed up for Stranger Things, Winona Ryder didn't have the faintest idea what Netflix or streaming was. Is this true or false?

(706) Which member of the Stranger Things cast is a music professor?

(707) What did Millie Bobby Brown NOT enjoy about the season one finale?

(708) What certificate does Dustin have on his wall in season two?

(709) What cruel nickname is Will Byers given at school in season two?

(710) The farm mailbox being destroyed when Hopper and Joyce escape from the Soviet enforcer in Stranger Things 3 is an Easter egg pertaining to which film?

(711) What is the name of the clown who gave Bob Newby childhood nightmares?

(712) Near the end of Stranger Things 3, Nancy shoots at Billy's speeding car. What movie scene is this a homage to?

(713) What song did Dacre Montgomery dance to in the Stranger Things audition tape he made?

(714) Which cast member was named the number one breakout star of 2016 by IMDB?

(715) The smiley faced yellow yo-yo used by Jonathan and Nancy to set a trap for the Demogorgon in season one is a reference to which film?

(716) Which character in Stranger Things was a Long Island waitress in the pilot script?

(717) What were the three main pop culture inspirations for the look of Billy Hargrove in Stranger Things?

(718) Nancy goes to a party at Tina's house in Stranger Things 2. In which 80s horror movie are characters named Nancy and Tina best friends?

(719) When Bob Newby puts the power back on in the lab, Hopper says "Son of a bitch did it." What film is this line taken from?

(720) What did the cover of the 1981 children's book Ronja Rövardotter by Astrid Lindgren inspire in Stranger Things 2?

(721) Which character has the second largest amount of lines in season one?

(722) Who is the tallest Stranger Things cast member?

(723) Jake Busey (who plays the sexist journalist Bruce) said that he had no idea he was even reading for Stranger Things 3 when he did his audition. Is this true or false?

(724) How long did it take to shoot the scenes in The Sauna Test where the kids trap Billy in the sauna?

(725) In the very early original plan for Stranger Things, season two was going to do a time jump to which year?

(726) Who ends up in a funfair hall of mirrors in season three?

(727) The first teaser for Stranger Things 3 includes a brief shot of which Tom Clancy novel?

(728) Where did the Flayer confront Billy at the start of season three?

(729) Does the character of Dr Brenner appear in season two?

(730) What happened to the DemoDog that Dustin put in the fridge at the end of Stranger Things 2?

(731) The Duffer Brothers said that they never actually played Dungeons & Dragons themselves despite it being such a major theme in the show. Is this statement true of false?

(732) Lucas wears the cap of an Italian cycling team (Ceramiche Ariostea) in Stranger Things 3. What film is this a reference to?

(733) What does Brenner have on his face in season four?

(734) How did Kali survive the 1979 Hawkins lab massacre?

(735) In season four we learn that the Upside Down seems to be frozen on a particular day. What day is this?

(736) How many languages can Robin speak?

(737) What do season four actors Joseph Quinn and Jamie Campbell Bower have in common?

(738) What is the name of the helicopter that Hopper, Joyce, and Murray hope can get them out of the Soviet Union in season four?

(739) What was in the cryptic package that Joyce receives in the mail early in season four?

(740) Where did Nancy and Jonathan work in season three?

(741) In which episode does Nancy Wheeler first venture into the Upside Down?

(742) In what month does Will Byers go missing in season one?

(743) The film Stand By Me is a big touchstone for Stranger Things. Which former Stranger Things cast member unsuccessfully auditioned for a lead role in Stand By Me?

(744) Why does Mike Wheeler jump off the quarry ledge in season one?

(745) What has Jonathan made for Will in the hospital at the end of season one?

(746) Music from a cult 1988 horror film can be heard when Dustin's toys come to life in the first episode of season three. Can you name this film?

(747) What brand of footwear does Steve Harrington wear in season one?

(748) Can you name the two episodes of Stranger Things which don't feature Eleven?

(749) Which member of the Stranger Things cast is a vegan?

ANSWERS TO QUESTIONS 700-749 ON PAGE 137

(750) What did Berry College in Atlanta double for in Stranger Things?

(751) In the Stranger Things 3 video game, what is Steve Harrington's weapon?

(752) In the episode E Pluribus Unum, the Flayer monster, with drooling teeth, hovers close to Nancy's face. What film is this a reference to?

(753) What is Eleven wearing when she is found in the woods by the boys in season one?

(754) In what sequence does Eleven get a rare double nosebleed?

(755) In which season four episode does Dr Sam Owens return to the show?

(756) In season four, we learn that Dr Owens got fired from his last job. Why did he get fired?

(757) How many lines does Millie Bobby Brown have as Eleven in season one?

(758) Which character did the Duffers say was the hardest to write on Stranger Things?

(759) Which member of the Stranger Things cast says that he is the only person in the show who has retained complete anonymity?

(760) Millie Bobby Brown got so fed up with Eleven's blonde wig in season one she once left it hanging in a tree. True or false?

(761) Who had to wear waterproof mascara in Stranger Things 3?

(762) What type of watch does Will Byers wear in season three?

(763) What is the name of the 1979 Russian science fiction film directed by Andrei Tarkovsky which influenced the look of the Upside Down in Stranger Things?

(764) In Stranger Things 3, Robin says "It is fascinating what 20 bucks will get you at the county recorders office. Starcourt Mall. The complete blueprints." What film is this a reference to?

(765) What type of car does Dustin's mother drive?

(766) Which character did the Duffers say they felt guilty about killing off?

(767) What is the name of the episode where Jonathan and Nancy spend the night together at Murray's house?

(768) Who is Stacey Albright in Stranger Things?

(769) What he is asked by Keith to name his top three films at the end of season three, what three movies does Steve Harrington choose?

(770) What is the name of the 1991 novel by Dan Simmons which was an influence on Stranger Things?

(771) Which movie inspired the scenes in season two where the Flayer infested Will Byers is tied to a chair?

(772) What inspired Troy's name in Stranger Things?

(773) Steve is given a truth serum in Stranger Things 3. What film is this a homage to?

(774) Why does Hopper feel guilty at the end of season one?

(775) Who ends up helping Jonathan and Nancy fight the Demogorgon in the season one finale?

(776) When do the boys in Stranger Things first learn that Eleven has super powers?

(777) Which three actors had to wear hairpieces in season two

because their own hair was too short to depict characters in the early 1980s?

(778) In what episode does Eleven shatter windows in Hopper's cabin?

(779) Why did David Harbour have to shave his head for Stranger Things 4?

(780) How many season four episodes does Suzie appear in?

(781) When was the mental hospital that features in Stranger Things 4 first mentioned in the show?

(782) What two Harry Potter universe films did Jamie Campbell Bower appear in?

(783) A soldier in Stranger Things 2 says "Stay frosty..." What film is this taken from?

(784) What does Alexei in season three do as a profession?

(785) What is the name of the European singer Steve Harrington's hair in season one was inspired by?

(786) What cartoon does Lucas have action figures from in season two?

(787) Who does Will Byers secretly have a crush on in Stranger Things 4?

(788) What name did Charlie Heaton have trouble saying in an American accent as Jonathan in Stranger Things?

(789) What brand of school folder does Barb have in season one?

(790) The spectacular sequence where Eleven makes the scientist van flip over the children on their bicycles in (the

season one episode) The Bathtub was very complicated and costly to shoot. How many times did this stunt have to be staged?

(791) The Duffers seriously considered bringing Barb back in season two. Is this true or false?

(792) When we see Hopper in his armchair early on in Stranger Things 3, what is he eating?

(793) Who attacks Hopper when he visits the Hawkins lab with Joyce at night in season three?

(794) The vintage song We'll Meet Again is heard in Stranger things 3. What film is this song most associated with?

(795) Joyce struggling with the two 'gate' keys in The Battle of Starcourt is a homage to which film?

(796) Which actress does Hopper joke that he wants a date with in season two?

(797) Besides waffles, what is in the 'Triple-Decker Eggo Extravaganza' that Hopper makes Eleven in season two?

(798) When Eleven is in Benny's diner in the first episode, what does she use her powers to turn off?

(799) In which season of the show does Joyce move out of Hawkins?

ANSWERS TO QUESTIONS 750-799 ON PAGE 140

(800) Which episode is the first season debut episode not to have the name of a character in its title?

(801) The lab intrigue in season one revolves around the

Department of Energy. What does the Department of Energy do in real life?

(802) David Harbour officiated a wedding in 2018 in his Hawkins police uniform. Is this true or false?

(803) What was Dr Owens called in the early season two scripts?

(804) Which character was described as a 'bullied overweight nerd' with spectacles in the original pitch notes?

(805) Why was Eleven's happy reaction to finally seeing Mike again in the penultimate episode of Stranger Things 2 an especially great piece of acting by Millie Bobby Brown?
(806) Why does Joyce's estranged husband visit Hawkins in season one?

(807) Which character has the most screentime in season three?

(808) When the pandemic shut down production on Stranger Things 4, Gaten Matarazzo volunteered as a food runner at a Long Beach Island restaurant. True or false?

(809) Who came up with the title Stranger Things as a name for the show?

(810) Who did Gaten Matarazzo say his favourite character in Stranger Things was?

(811) What is the scene in Stranger Things 2 where Steve and Dustin gaze down the tunnel created by the escaped Dart a homage to?

(812) What type of music is the Stranger Things score?

(813) Which character in Stranger Things has the most screentime in the first three seasons when they are tallied

together?

(814) What is the name of the famous 1980s science fiction miniseries about blood drinking aliens that Robert Englund appeared in?

(815) Where is the portal that Steve's gang use to escape from the Upside Down in season four located? They also later use this portal to ENTER the Upside Down.

(816) What do Vecna's murders open in our reality?

(817) What was the real life 'Satanic Panic' which plays a big part in the story of Stranger Things 4?

(818) What is the number of the 'special' child that Brenner does a test with in the prologue to the first episode of season four?

(819) How long was the gap between seasons three and four being released?

(820) What two famous people inspired the teacher Scott Clarke's name?

(821) How many heads does the Demogorgon in Dungeons & Dragons have?

(822) Can you name three titles that the Duffers considered calling the show before they settled on Stranger Things?

(823) Which member of the Stranger Things cast briefly held up the production on season one when they turned up one morning covered in gold glitter?

(824) Which member of the cast lost his voice because of all the screaming he had to do in the season two finale?

(825) Where did Shannon Purser film her Stranger Things

audition tape?

(826) Who had to be asked for permission for the boys to wear Ghostbusters costumes in season two?

(827) For the climax of The Spy, Will informs the scientists of where he thinks the Mind Flayer is hiding and they send soldiers scurrying into the tunnels. What is this sequence a homage to?

(828) Which members of the cast said they nearly gave up acting before Stranger Things came along?

(829) Can you name the Steven Spielberg film Noah Schnapp appeared in before Stranger Things?

(830) How old was Joe Keery when he was cast as Steve Harrington?

(831) Season one of Strangers Things is partly inspired by MKUltra. What was MKUltra?

(832) What is the name of the science fiction horror film the Duffer Brothers directed before Stranger Things made them famous?

(833) Which scene in season two included real childhood photographs of Shannon Purser?

(834) Near the end of the season one finale, Dustin has to carry the exhausted Eleven into the classroom. Which character was originally supposed to carry Eleven?

(835) What does the Butts County Probate Court double for in Stranger Things?

(836) Which member of the cast claimed it was his idea to have a video game arcade in season two?

(837) Who did Peggy Miley play in season three?

(838) In what specific location is Will Byers rescued from the Upside Down in season one?

(839) What beverage does Lucas compare John Carpenter's The Thing and The Thing From Another World to in season three?

(840) What does Dustin spray Lucas with in Stranger Things 3 after Eleven spooks him by making his toys come to life as a prank?

(841) Who wears a vintage Le Tigre polo shirt in season one?

(842) How many seasons does Kali appear in?

(843) What was the first season of the show where all the scripts were completed before shooting began?

(844) What television cooking show did Millie Bobby Brown appear on before she was famous?

(845) What was the inspiration for the title of the season three episode The Mall Rats?

(846) In which season four episode does Hopper escape from prison for the first time?

(847) In what episode do Nancy and Robin team up for the first time?

(848) What goof did the Duffers make concerning Will Byers in the season four roller rink scenes?

(849) What is the first season of the show where Eleven doesn't eat any Eggos?

ANSWERS TO QUESTIONS 800-849 ON

(850) What does Dustin offer Nancy in the first ever episode before she shuts her bedroom door on him?

(851) The house of Heather the lifeguard in Stranger Things 3 is deliberately similar to a house in a 1980s horror film. Can you name the film?

(852) Why did the Duffer Brothers say they killed Benny and Barb so early in the show?

(853) What is the name of the medical drama Millie Bobby Brown appeared in when she was still an unknown child actor?

(854) Which main cast regulars in Stranger Things have been in music bands?

(855) Patrick Henry Academy at 109 S. Lee St. in Stockbridge was the location for Hawkins High/Middle School in Stranger Things. Why did this school close down in real life?

(856) What does Joyce buy Will for Christmas in season one?

(857) In Stranger Things 2, you can see a periodic table on a school classroom wall. What is wrong with this periodic table?

(858) What is the name of the Stephen King story about a girl with powerful telekinetic abilities which was one of the many influences on Stranger Things?

(859) In what year was Mike Wheeler born?

(860) Which famous literary estate was Dungeons & Dragons subject to legal action from?

(861) Which animated character is Alexei is a fan of in season three?

(862) What scene from the show did Joe Keery have to do for his Stranger Things audition?

(863) What movie scene is the military corridor battle in the missile silo in Papa a homage to?

(864) Hopper is called a "Fat Rambo" in Stranger Things 3. What is the name of the Rambo film which came out the same year Stranger Things 3 is set?

(865) Who asked the Duffers for Eleven and Max to be friends in season three?

(866) Where exactly are Hopper and Eleven finally reunited in season four?

(867) What did the building used for the Hawkins Department of Energy building exterior in Stranger Things used to be?

(868) What does Erica sarcastically call her vent crawling mission in Stranger Things 3?

(869) The bus number Eleven takes to find Kali/Eight in The Lost Sister is the 422. What is the significance of these numbers?

(870) Why is Eleven the only child in the Hawkins lab in season one?

(871) The special effects on season one were only completed days before Stranger Things was due to begin streaming on Netflix. True or false?

(872) When she decides to go away with Dr Owens to get her powers back in season four, Eleven leaves a note for Mike. What does she say in the note?

(873) In which season four episode does Robin find it hard to walk because she has to wear high heels?

(874) How many seasons did the school bully Troy and his sidekick appear in?

(875) What does Dustin, much to the annoyance of Mr Wheeler, help himself to at breakfast in The Nina Project?

(876) Why did Caleb McLaughlin ask for Lucas to have number eight as his basketball number?

(877) What brand of shoebox does Eleven have her school presentation in at the start of Stranger Things 4?

(878) Why does Eddie go back into the Upside Down again in the finale?

(879) Where does Eddie mostly hide in season four when he goes on the run?

(880) In season one, Hopper has to search through a swathe of microfiche in the library to research the Hawkins lab. What is microfiche?

(881) Which Steven Spielberg film did Millie Bobby Brown unsuccessfully audition for before Stranger Things?

(882) Which Stranger Things star briefly lived in commune as a child with no electricity?

(883) Why is Bob Newby choosing to watch the film Mr Mom at Halloween an in-joke?

(884) What production headache arose when they did the car chase at the start of season two?

(885) What did Joe Keery and Dacre Montgomery both have to do some training for in preparation for season two?

(886) What is the name of Suzie's younger brother who keeps turning the power off and firing plastic arrows at people?

(887) What did Maya Hawke do the day Stranger Things 3 was released?

(888) Who did twins Charlotte and Clara Ward play in Stranger Things?

(889) What is the name of the older sister of Suzie that Argyle has a crush on?

(890) What is the name of the Hawkins gun and weapons store in Stranger Things 4?

(891) What is the name of famous sitcom we see both Eleven and Joyce watching at different times in Stranger Things?

(892) What did Noah Schnapp research in preparation for Stranger Things 2?

(893) How many auditions did Caleb McLaughlin have to do before he was given the part of Lucas?

(894) When Hopper wakes up in his trailer in season one, after being knocked out by agents at the Hawkins lab, he ransacks his home searching for listening devices that he suspects they have planted. What film is this a homage to?

(896) In which season does Dustin wear a Castroville Artichoke Festival t-shirt?

(897) When was Millie Bobby Brown told she would have to cut her hair to play Eleven?

(898) How many children were competing with Gaten Matarazzo for the part of Dustin?

(899) The Lost Sister episode features graffiti which references a Grant Morrison comic book. What is the name of this comic book?

ANSWERS TO QUESTIONS 850-899 ON PAGE 148

(900) Which 1980s Stanley Kubrick film is Matthew Modine most famous for?

(901) In Stranger Things 2, Max has a surfing film poster on her wall. What is the name of the film?

(902) The alley fight between Jonathan Steve in season one is a homage to which John Carpenter film?

(903) Stranger Things 3 includes a blast of Neutron Dance by The Pointer Sisters. What famous film did this song feature in?

(904) What does E Pluribus unum mean?

(905) We we see a lab scientist enter the Upside Down in season one but he doesn't survive for very long. What is the name of this scientist?

(906) Which famous English football team does Millie Bobby Brown support?

(907) Which character ends season four in a coma?

(908) The diner owner Benny was originally supposed to be a relative of Dustin. Is this true or false?

(909) How many rats were used in the production of Stranger Things 3?

(910) What did Millie Bobby Brown suffer from when shooting the season two finale cage sequence?

(911) Which film does Mr Clarke have a tombstone from on his town model in season three?

(912) Can you name the Clive Barker film which the Duffers featured in their pitch booklet for Stranger Things?

(913) What had to be applied to Sadie Sink in season two?

(914) Out of the four main boys in Strangers Things, which two have never ventured into the Upside Down?

(915) What movie set is the interior of the Wheeler house based on?

(916) Who nearly skipped the Stranger Things auditions because he wasn't in the mood to go after a slew of rejections for other parts?

(917) Which two cast members went on a family vacation together after production on season two ended?

(918) Which member of the Stranger Things cast recently directed his first short film?

(919) When Steve and Robin are recovering from the effects of the Soviet truth serum in Stranger Things 3, music from a 1980s movie can be heard. Can you name this movie?

(920) Which character wears a camouflage bandana in season one?

(921) The singer Limahl was a big fan of Stranger Things even before they used his Neverending Story song. Is this statement true or false?

(922) What 1980s movie are the costumes of Steve, Robin, and Nancy inspired by when they venture into the Upside Down in the season four finale?

(923) Where do Jason Carver and the Hawkins Tigers basketball team hang out in Stranger Things 4?

(924) Can you name the JJ Abrams film which was an influence on Stranger Things?

(925) What famous line of toys is Erica Sinclair a fan of in season three?

(926) Can you name the two characters who were NOT killed in the same season they were introduced?

(927) What is the name of the season four episode where Eleven first finds out that Dr Brenner is still alive?

(928) In which season of the show is the lab and Eleven's backstory not a major part of the plot?

(929) What song plays at the end of the season two finale?

(930) Millie Bobby Brown said that eating waffles as Eleven in season one was a bit of an ordeal. What reason did she cite for this?

(931) Steve's costume at Scoops Ahoy in season three has a holster. What is the holster for?

(932) How many times did Millie Bobby Brown lose her voice shooting Stranger Things 3?

(933) In the Family Video store, at the end of Stranger Things 3, you can just about make out a poster for Private School - a 1983 teen comedy. What connects Private School to Stranger Things?

(934) Why did Noah Schnapp think his Stranger Things audition was terrible?

(935) Who was child actor Martie Marie Blair the body double for in season four?

(936) What real life conspiracy theory was an influence on

Stranger Things?

(937) How does Robin work out where 'Reefer Rick' lives in Stranger Things 4?

(938) In which country did Stranger Things go viral the quickest?

(939) It was always planned in the show for Steve and Dustin to team up and become friends. Is this statement true or false?

(940) What did Brett Gelman have to take classes in to play Murray in season three?

(941) What scene in season three did Millie Bobby Brown say she did some method acting for?

(942) In a strange quirk of casting coincidence, David Harbour also played an inmate in a Russian prison for a movie around the time of Stranger Things 4. Can you name the movie?

(943) Gaten Matarazzo said that he had never even seen The Neverending Story before the production of Stranger Things 3. Is this statement true or false?

(944) What did Noah Schnapp say his favourite ever scene in Stranger Things was?

(945) How much money do Joyce and Murray have to take to Alaska in season four as part of the plan to release Hopper?

(946) In the episode Vecna's Curse, Max mentions Ted Bundy. Who was Ted Bundy?

(947) What car does Mayor Kline drive?

(948) Where were the beach scenes in Stranger Things 3 shot?

(949) In which movie did Millie Bobby Brown make her film

debut?

ANSWERS TO QUESTIONS 900-949 ON PAGE 151

(950) What does Erica request in return for crawling through the vent in Stranger Things 3?

(951) In the episode The Flayed, The Soviet enforcer says to Hopper - "You're a policeman. Policemen have rules." What film is this line taken from?

(952) What violent thing does Eleven do to the local mean girl at the roller rink in Vecna's Curse?

(953) Eleven throws a car at the Soviet baddies in the mall in season three. Can you name what sort of car it was?

(954) Where does the scene that introduces us to Eddie Munson in season four take place?

(955) Who is the wealthiest member of the Stranger Things cast?

(956) When Alexei is at the fair in Stranger Things 3, you can see some Fraggle figures as prizes. What television show are Fraggles from?

(957) What was the first season of Stranger Things where all the episodes were not released at once to stream?

(958) What is the first episode in season four where Joyce and Eleven actually speak to each other?

(959) What family owns the abandoned mill in Stranger Things 3?

(960) What television show is Easter egged when Will Byers

stares into the bathroom mirror at the end of the first season?

(961) What food do Dr Owens and Eleven order in the diner in The Monster and the Superhero?

(962) In which episode in season four does Eleven show the first sign of her powers returning?

(963) In the dubbed French language version of Stranger Things, Lucas is voiced in the first season by a woman. Is this true or false?

(964) Which episode do voters on Ranker rank as the greatest ever Stranger Things episode?

(965) What is the name of the real town which doubles for Hawkins?

(966) What does Dr Brenner do during breakfast in the prologue to the The Hellfire Club?

(967) What famous 1980s movie did Matthew Modine turn down the lead role in?

(968) What Jim Henson film does Suzie have a poster for on her wall in season three?

(969) Eleven has a photograph by her bed in season three. What is in the photograph?

(970) Which cast member combined appearing in the early seasons of Stranger Things with being a student at New York University?

(971) What is the lowest rated episode of season three on IMDB?

(972) What does Murray cook for dinner when he turns up at the Byers house in The Monster and the Superhero?

(973) The way the monster in Stranger Things 3 can melt down and reform into a bigger mass is evocative of which 1990s movie character?

(974) What is the name of the detective with famous relatives that Millie Bobby Brown plays away from Stranger Things?

(975) What has Eleven made for her school project at the start of Stranger Things 4?

(976) What is written on the wall when Dustin locates Dart in the school toilets in Stranger Things 2?

(977) Which two Stranger Things cast members both said they would like to play Spider-Man?

(978) The song Higher and Higher by Jackie Wilson features in The Battle of Starcourt. What movie is this song most famous for appearing in?

(979) What are names of the two agents assigned to protect the Byers home in season four?

(980) What does Argyle's 'try before you deny' refrain refer to?

(981) What do Steve's gang steal in the season four episode Papa?

(982) What happened to Brenner the last time we saw him in season one?

(983) In season one, Eleven wears a Polly Flanders style dress to go to the school with the boys. Who is the original owner of this dress?

(984) Who does Lucas have a fight with in the season four finale?

(985) Eleven wears a baby mask in season two. What film is

this mask from?

(986) In which season does Steve first become a babysitter to the kids?

(987) In the original plan for Stranger Things 2, how was Bob going to die?

(988) What is the name of the room in the Hawkins lab where the children play games?

(989) How many times does Hopper escape from prison in season four?

(990) The Claremont House is a Gothic Victorian style house built in 1882. Which house does the Claremont House double for in Stranger Things?

(991) Which cast member from the show was accepted into a college in 2022?

(992) How much did the costume department say Eleven's blonde wig in season one cost?

(993) In 2016, Time Out reported that Hawkins in Stranger Things had won their poll of the fictional town where readers would most like to go on holiday. Can you guess which fictional places came second and third?

(994) What does Dr Brenner request from Eleven when he is dying?

(995) What brand of sneakers does Eleven wear in Stranger Things 3?

(996) What object do the victims of Vecna always see in their visions when under his curse?

(997) In what episode of season two was Bob originally going

to die?

(998) The scene where Hopper manages to obtain a Soviet uniform in the underground base in the finale of Stranger Things 3 is a homage to which scene in which film?

(999) Steve's basketball scenes in Stranger Things 2 use the song Push IT to the Limit. What famous movie did this song feature in?

(1000) What is the name of the book Lucas is reading to Max in the hospital at the end of season four?

ANSWERS TO QUESTIONS 950-1000 ON PAGE 155

ANSWERS

(1) Ross Duffer and Matt Duffer.

(2) Hopper's daughter was named Sara.

(3) Forest Hills

(4) Mike Wheeler was the first character to use the term 'Upside Down'.

(5) Suzie's computer is a Commodore Amiga.

(6) Barbara Holland

(7) The film playing at the mall cinema is 1985's Day of the Dead. Day of the Dead was the conclusion of George A Romero's famous zombie trilogy and followed on from Night of the Living Dead (1968) and Dawn of the Dead (1978).

(8) Dungeons & Dragons was invented in 1974 by Gary Gygax and Dave Arneson.

(9) Chrissy Cunningham

(10) Lenora Hills

(11) Benguiat. This typeface is heavily associated with Stephen King paperbacks from the 1980s.

(12) Stranger Things was originally titled Montauk. Montauk is a hamlet at the east end of the Long Island peninsula and famed for its beaches. Ross and Matt Duffer were very inspired by Steven Spielberg's classic movie Jaws in their early plans for the show. They decided not to have the show set in Montauk in the end because they feared that shooting on the coast might pose too many logistical problems.

(13) Three. Paul Reiser was in Aliens, Winona Ryder was in Alien: Resurrection, and Amy Seimetz (who played Becky Ives in Stranger Things) was in Alien: Covenant.

(14) Samantha has actually come as Siouxsie Sioux - the lead singer of Siouxsie and the Banshees.

(15) Eddie plays Metallica's Master of Puppets.

(16) Mike Wheeler has the most lines out of any character in season one.

(17) The Eggo waffle brand was invented in San Jose, California, by Tony, Sam, and Frank Dorsa in 1953. The Eggo brand was purchased by the Kellogg Company in 1968.

(18) Hawkins is located in Roane County. Both of these places are obviously fictional.

(19) Canada. Finn Wolfhard was born in Vancouver, British Columbia, Canada, in 2002.

(20) The Palace Arcade in Stranger Things 2 is named after the 20 Grand Palace Arcade in the 1983 fantasy film WarGames. WarGames stars Matthew Broderick as a whizz-kid hacker teen who nearly starts World War III on his computer.

(21) Dustin feeds his new pet 'Dart' 3 Musketeers candy. 3 Musketeers is a candy bar made by Mars, Incorporated. Introduced in 1932, it is a candy bar consisting of chocolate-covered fluffy whipped nougat. In Europe you might know this as a Milky Way.

(22) Hopper reads Anne of Green Gables to Eleven in the cabin in season two. We saw him read this book to his daughter in season one flashbacks. Anne of Green Gables is a 1908 novel by Canadian author Lucy Maud Montgomery (published as L. M. Montgomery). The book is about an eleven year-old orphan named Anne Shirley.

(23) In Stranger Things 2, Will tells Dr Owens that Reese's Pieces is his preferred candy. Reese's Pieces are a peanut butter and chocolate candy introduced in 1977. They became very popular with the 1982 release of E.T. the Extra-Terrestrial, in which the candy is featured.

(24) Dr Brenner's first name is Martin.

(25) Eleven bleeds from the left nostril when she uses her powers.

(26) HPL is a reference to the horror writer H.P. Lovecraft. Lovecraft's stories are often about inexplicable creatures, alternate dimensions, and forces we can't possibly understand. His work was a big influence on Stranger Things.

(27) Stranger Things 4 takes place in 1986.

(28) Steve and Robin's sailor suits at Scoops Ahoy owe much to the Captain Hook Fish & Chip scenes in Fast Times at Ridgemont High. Fast Times at Ridgemont High is a 1982 teen comedy film which has woven its way into the subtext of Stranger Things many times.

(29) Rink-O-Mania

(30) Dustin Henderson has the most lines out of any character in season two.

(31) Troy's full name is Troy Walsh.

(32) Dustin Henderson is the only one of the boys who doesn't have any siblings.

(33) Max has the same skateboard as Marty McFly in Back to the future.

(34) The Clash. The song appeared on their 1982 album Combat Rock.

(35) Agent Connie Frazier

(36) Sadie Sink as Max Mayfield joined the show in season two.

(37) Alex P Keaton was the name of Michael J Fox's character in the popular eighties sitcom Family Ties. This is why Steve keeps referring to Marty McFly as Alex P Keaton in Stranger Things 3. Family Ties was what Michael J Fox was most famous for at the time.

(38) Jason Carver.

(39) Stranger Things 3 has characters drinking New Coke. In 1985 Coca-Cola was rebranded as New Coke and the formula tweaked to make it sweeter and more syrupy like Pepsi. There were (famously) howls of protests from people who liked Coca-Cola exactly as it was and didn't understand why it had to change. The old formula was eventually brought back and the company lost tens of millions of dollars in unsold bottles of New Coke.

(40) Deputy Powell and Deputy Callahan. Powell becomes the chief of police in Stranger Things 4 when Hopper is presumed dead.

(41) Hopper likes Schlitz beer. In the 80s this was known as cheap beer.

(42) The cinema in Hawkins is showing the Tom Cruise film All the Right Moves in season one.

(43) Sean Astin originally auditioned for the part of Murray Bauman.

(44) Benny gives Eleven some strawberry ice cream in The Vanishing of Will Byers.

(45) Operation Mirkwood. Mirkwood appears in the writings

of J.R.R. Tolkein. It is a great forest in Middle-earth located in the eastern region of Rhovanion between the Grey Mountains and Gondor.

(46) Thriller by Michael Jackson features in the Stranger Things 2 trailer. It was not so much Michael Jackson the producers wanted but the atmospheric intro and the opening narration by the legendary horror icon Vincent Price.

(47) 307 girls read for the part of Eleven before Millie was given the role.

(48) Robin's full name is Robin Buckley.

(49) Mike and Nancy's parents are named Ted and Karen.

(50) Tangerine Dream. Tangerine Dream is a German electronic music band founded in 1967 by Edgar Froese. They composed the scores for films like Sorcerer, Thief, Risky Business, The Keep, Firestarter, Legend, Three O'Clock High, Near Dark, Shy People, and Miracle Mile. Songs by Tangerie Dream have been included in the Stranger Things score.

(51) Florence (Flo) is the name of the dry witted no nonsense secretary at the Hawkins police station.

(52) Dustin is after the school supply of chocolate pudding.

(53) Mike's plane landing mimics the orange skied shot of John McClane's plane landing in California at the start of Die Hard.

(54) Eleven levitates a Millennium Falcon model.

(55) The Evil Dead

(56) Millie Bobby Brown

(57) Chester. The dog did not return for season two. David

Harbour said the dog was not very well trained and didn't do what it was told. This would explain why Chester didn't come back.

(58) Before he turned his hand to acting, Charlie Heaton was the drummer in a rock band called Comanechi.

(59) Bob Newby works for Radioshack in season two. RadioShack, formerly RadioShack Corporation, is an American retailer founded in 1921. Radioshack was a big cheese in the electronics world - even as late as the 1990s.

(60) Gaten Matarazzo was the first of the kids to be cast in Stranger Things.

(61) Chicago

(62) Farrah Fawcett. The Charlie's Angels actress had a range of hair care products named after her by Fabergé Organics in the early eighties. Steve won't be happy to learn though that the Farrah Fawcett range of products ended in 1984.

(63) Dragon's Lair. Dragon's Lair is a laserdisc video game released in 1983. Dragon's Lair was something new at the time. Rather than graphics it had Disney style animation by Don Bluth. You play Dirk the Daring, a knight trying to rescue Princess Daphne from a dragon. The drawback to Dragon's Lair was that you had no control over the action. It was more like a 'choose your own adventure book'. You make a choice and then the animation plays out and you see if your course of action got Dirk killed or not. Subsequently, it didn't have long lasting appeal as you either learned the pattern or grew frustrated at watching Dirk get killed for 50 cents a time. When it first appeared though, Dragon's Lair was something of a short lived phenomenon. Dustin is clearly obsessed with the game in Stranger Things 2 although he seems to be entering the frustration stage.

(64) The Upside Down was called the 'Nether' in the original

scripts. At some point they simply decided that the Upside Down sounded better.

(65) The password to enter Will's woodland clubhouse 'Castle Byers' is Radagast. Radagast is a wizard in Lord of the Rings.

(66) The twins also played baby Judith in season four of The Walking Dead.

(67) Georgia. Much of the shooting takes place in Atlanta and the surrounding area.

(68) Promethium is the substance used to create Cyborg in DC Comics.

(69) 1981's Halloween II. Halloween II picks up right where Halloween ends. Laurie Strode (Jamie Lee Curtis) is rushed to hospital as Michael Myers is on the loose again in Haddonfield after somehow surviving being shot by Dr Loomis (Donald Pleasance). Michael eventually realises Laurie is at the hospital and goes there, killing most of the staff in the process. As ever, Dr Loomis is on the bogeyman's trail.

(70) "Men of science have made abundant mistakes of every kind" is a quote by George Sarton. George Alfred Leon Sarton was a famous Belgian scientist.

(71) Dear Billy

(72) Kyle Lambert

(73) Kali's powers are that she can trigger hallucinations in people and so project a fake reality.

(74) Kentucky Fried Chicken. Steve refers to it as KFC - although at the time (1984) Kentucky Fried Chicken had yet to rebrand themselves as KFC.

(75) The kids! The Duffers said that networks didn't like the

idea of a show with children as main characters and wanted them to dump the kids. Thankfully, this didn't happen in the end. It was the kids that made the show so popular.

(76) Millie said the fries were stone cold and therefore not very nice. She did have a spit bucket though.

(77) Weathertop. This is a direct reference to Lord of the Rings: The Fellowship of the Ring. It's the hill where Frodo is stabbed by the chief Nazgul. In Elvish, Weathertop is Amon Sul. It was destroyed during the kingdom of Arthedain's war with Angmar.

(78) Billy Hargrove has a Camaro in seasons two and three. This is the car the baddie Buddy Repperton drives in Christine (a Stephen King book made into a film by John Carpenter).

(79) Millie added 'Bobby' to her name to distinguish herself online from a controversial performance artist also named Millie Brown.

(80) The season four finale The Piggyback required the most special effects.

(81) Caleb McLaughlin (who plays Lucas) is the oldest of the 'kids' in the cast. He was born in October, 2001.

(82) Family Video. Family Video still exists to this day.

(83) Stranger Texts.

(84) At the Halloween party in season two, Nancy and Steve are dressed as Tom Cruise and Rebecca De Mornay in Risky Business.

(85) Elfen Lied. Elfen Lied is a manga series and later anime. Elfen Lied is about a mutant 'Diclonius' girl named Lucy who has telekinetic powers and escapes from a military facility. It has some very obvious parallels with Stranger Things and was

cited as one of the influences on Eleven by the creators of the show.

(86) Kamchatka - a Soviet peninsula located in Russia.

(87) Kajagoogoo

(88) The Mist. This story was later adapted into a pretty good Frank Darabont film.

(89) The Hellfire Club is the name of a secret society in the X-Men comics. It plays a key role in the Dark Phoenix storyline - which was one of but many inspirations for Eleven. The Dark Phoenix Saga is a comic by Chris Claremont and John Byrne that collects together X-Men #129-137. The comic is referenced in Stranger Things season one.

(90) Lithuania

(91) Debbie Harry was the lead singer of punkish pop band Blondie.

(92) Dr Sam Owens supplied Hopper with a birth certificate for Eleven.

(93) Silent Hill. The ghostly mist engulfed town of Silent Hill was an obvious influence on Stranger Things.

(94) Claudia Henderson

(95) Brenner was known simply as Agent One in the pilot script. He wasn't called Brenner until later on.

(96) Dustin's turtle is named Yertle. Yertle is a character in the television series The Wubbulous World of Dr Seuss.

(97) Eleven's real name is Jane Ives. She goes by the name Jane Hopper now though. Her full name is therefore Jane Ives Hopper.

(98) Jim Hopper is the character with the most lines in season three.

(99) The translation of the morse code is "us".

(100) The Twilight Zone episode is called Little Girl Lost. Little Girl Lost is about a child who becomes trapped in another dimension after entering a portal which opened in her bedroom.

(101) Gaten Matarazzo, Caleb McLaughlin and Sadie Sink vaguely knew each other before Stranger Things from working in shows on Broadway. Winona Ryder knew Matthew Modine because they'd appeared in a Roy Orbison music video together. Winona also knew Cary Elwes because they were both in Francis Ford Coppola's Dracula film in the early 1990s.

(102) Noah Schnapp (as Will Byers) was the last of the kids to be cast.

(103) "It's a trap!" is the exact quote that Admiral Ackbar famously declares in Return of the Jedi during the space battle.

(104) Netflix began in 1997. In the early days of the company they were a DVD rental business. They began producing their own content in 2013.

(105) Charlie Heaton and Natalia Dyer became a real couple after playing Jonathan and Nancy in Stranger Things.

(106) Wayward Pines

(107) The Snow Ball dance is first mentioned in the season one finale The Upside Down. Mike mentions the dance to Eleven while they are hiding at the school.

(108) Robin names The Apartment (1960), Children of Paradise (1945), and The Hidden Fortress (1958) as her

favourite movies.

(109) Bob the Brain.

(110) Eleven banished Ballard to the Upside Down - and thus created Vecna - in 1979.

(111) Dustin names his radio tower 'Cerebro' after the device Professor X uses to track mutants in The X-Men.

(112) The Lost Sister is the lowest rated episode of Stranger Things on IMBD.

(113) Millie Bobby Brown

(114) The Cold War was actually on its last legs in 1985 when Stranger Things 3 takes place. The Soviet Union would only last until 1991.

(115) Michael Stein and Kyle Dixon.

(116) Erica was introduced in Stranger Things 2.

(117) Suzie is reading Ursula K. Le Guin's children's fantasy book A Wizard Of Earthsea.

(118) Bradley's Big Buy

(119) Argyle is the name of John McClane's limo driver in Die Hard.

(120) Stranger Things 2 and Stranger Things 4. Both of these seasons had nine episodes rather than eight.

(121) Keith is always eating Cheetos.

(122) Ruth, Nevada.

(123) Papa

(124) Marissa

(125) Gwinnett Place Mall. Gwinnett Place Mall was an abandoned and derelict mall that sat on the outskirts of Atlanta. Gwinnett Place Mall was first operational in 1984 but had been empty and closed for a few years when the Stranger Things team found it. Stranger Things production designer Chris Trujillo and a team of eighty people spent six weeks renovating Gwinnett Place Mall by restoring the facades and signs, cleaning the place up, adding lights, and putting in operational stores and a food court.

(126) Sadie Sink's sister Jacey was used as the younger version of Max in the flashbacks.

(127) Terry Ives

(128) James

(129) True. Steve was indeed going to be killed off in season one. The Duffers liked the performance of Joe Keery though so they gave Steve a redemptive arc and kept him in the show.

(130) Mike and Eleven meet for the first time at the end of the first ever episode (The Vanishing of Will Byers) when the boys are out in the woods looking for Will and instead encounter Eleven in the rain.

(131) Bob is killed by DemoDogs after restoring the power at the Hawkins lab.

(132) Lt. Colonel Jack Sullivan

(133) Gold Leader is the callsign of Lando Calrissian in Return of the Jedi.

(134) Noah Schnapp is the youngest of the 'kids' in the cast. He was born in October, 2004.

(135) The state trooper is reading Stephen King's Cujo.

(136) Vickie is name of the girl that Robin has a crush on in season four.

(137) Victor is being held at Pennhurst Mental Hospital.

(138) Dig Dug. Dig Dug is Japanese arcade game from 1982. The game involves a character named Dig Dug who digs tunnels in the dirt and has to avoid monsters.

(139) The void of nothingness that Eleven enters in Stranger Things was influenced by Under the Skin. Under the Skin is a 2013 film with Scarlett Johansson as an alien who preys on victims in a void of nothing with a liquid floor.

(140) Benny's Burgers is really Tiffany's Kitchen in Lithia Springs, Georgia. This is a real diner that you can visit and eat in.

(141) Dacre Montgomery is Australian.

(142) Steve and Dustin's double act began in the season two episode Dig Dug.

(143) Joe Keery originally auditioned for the part of Jonathan Byers.

(144) The Terminator

(145) Hopper's tropical shirt in season three is inspired by Tom Selleck's casual wardrobe on the eighties private investigator action detective show Magnum.

(146) Noah Schnapp initially auditioned for the part of Mike Wheeler.

(147) Barb is sitting by the swimming pool at Steve Harrington's house when the Demogorgon strikes.

(149) The boys pretend Eleven is their cousin from Sweden!

(150) This is a reference to the pie eating contest sequence in the 1986 film Stand By Me.

(151) Millie only says 246 words as Eleven in the first season of Stranger Things.

(152) Hawkins and Hopper are characters in the 1987 film Predator.

(153) Robert Englund is most famous for playing Freddy Krueger in the Nightmare on Elm Street horror franchise (which began in 1984).

(154) Dustin's sneakers in the first season are K-Swiss Heaven S.

(155) This is the camera that Doc Brown uses in Back to the Future.

(156) The Duffers thought that the best episode in season one was The Bathtub. They loved this episode the most because it brought all of the characters together for the first time.

(157) Hopper's trailer home in season one was purchased by the production staff for the paltry sum of one dollar.

(158) The Dark Crystal

(159) Max dresses up as Michael Myers from the Halloween franchise in Stranger Things 2.

(160) Jonathan rents Mr Mom, WarGames, and Twilight Zone: The Movie.

(161) Stand By Me and E.T. the Extra-Terrestrial.

(162) Dustin's elaborate bequiffed hair at the Snow Ball dance

in Stranger Things 2 is a reference to Philip "Duckie" Dale (Jon Cryer) in the John Hughes movie Pretty in Pink.

(163) The Duffers said that Eleven was the hardest character to cast in season one. The main reason for this is that child actors often find it hard to stay in character when they don't have much dialogue and often have to remain silent. The Duffers saw that Millie Bobby Brown was clearly able to sustain the same level of focus at all times.

(164) This is a reference to the 1975 film Death Race 2000. In that film a totalitarian regime creates a violent car race where you get points for running over pedestrians.

(165) Converse

(166) Millie and Charlie are both British.

(167) Brahms' Lullaby

(168) Eleven spends most of season one living in Mike's basement.

(169) Maya's parents are the actors Ethan Hawke and Uma Thurman.

(170) Escape from New York

(171) Francesca Reale originally auditioned for the part of Robin.

(172) Argyle works at Surfer Boy Pizza.

(173) Fred Benson

(174) Mike and Eleven are finally reunited at the end of The Mind Flayer - which is the penultimate episode of Stranger Things 2.

(175) Nancy dances with Dustin after she notices he has no one to dance with.

(176) Back to the Future

(177) Joe Keery and Noah Schnapp were upgraded to full recurring cast members for Stranger Things 2.

(178) Gabriella Pizzolo and Gaten both have a Broadway background. In 2013, Gabriella Pizzolo became one of the many girls who took turns playing Matilda on Broadway and in 2015 took on her most notable stage role yet — Young Alison in the Tony-Award winning production of Fun Home. Before earning her Broadway debut, she appeared in several regional productions of plays like Les Miserables, Ragtime, and Miracle on 34th Street starting at the age of seven.

(179) False. Priah said she had never actually watched Stranger Things before her audition.

(180) It. Finn played Richie Tozier in the film. This Stephen King adaptation is about small town kids who must band together to fight an inexplicable evil - which manifests itself in the form of a creepy clown. Finn later shot Stranger Things 3 and the It sequel at the same time.

(181) Millie was born in Spain.

(182) Finn had to tape his audition in bed because he was sick at the time.

(183) Millie auditioned for the part of Laura/X-23 in the Hugh Jackman film Logan but lost out to Dafne Keen.

(184) True. Millie said that, because her hearing is quite poor, they have to have someone right next to her say action when she does a scene.

(185) Alexei is partial to a cherry Slurpee.

(186) Max is originally from California.

(187) Eleven's powers seem to be activated again in The Massacre at Hawkins Lab when she remembers the true events of 1979 while in the sensory deprivation tank. We only see evidence for this though in the next episode - Papa.

(188) Suzie lives in Salt Lake City.

(189) The first teaser for Stranger Things 3 arrived in the form of a Starcourt Mall infomercial.

(190) Lucas uses a wrist-rocket (slingshot).

(191) Murray was introduced in season two.

(192) Eleven levitates the NINA sensory deprivation chamber.

(193) The Stranger Things kids handed out peanut butter and jelly sandwiches to celebrities at the 2016 Emmy awards.

(194) Season three. Stranger Things 3 is set during the summer so the kids are on their summer break from school.

(195) The background music is the drinking song from Giuseppe Verdi's La Traviata.

(196) True. Matthew Modine initially thought Dr Brenner was too vague as a character and declined the part.

(197) Sadie had to learn how to use a skateboard.

(198) Camp Know Where.

(199) True. Gaten Matarazzo did indeed read for the parts of Lucas and Mike.

(200) Mr Clarke is at home watching John Carpenter's The Thing.

(201) The car that Hopper steals at the gas station in Stranger Things 3 is a Cadillac Eldorado Biarritz.

(202) Pollywog, Frogogorgon, Catogorgon, DemoDog, and Demogorgon.

(203) Pittsburgh

(204) The season one finale The Upside Down. Mike kisses Eleven on the cheek in this episode.

(205) Holly Wheeler is made to look like Drew Barrymore's Gertie from E.T. in season one.

(206) The Demogorgon made its first Dungeons & Dragons appearance in the 1976 game Eldritch Wizardry.

(207) Stranger Things 4 is the first season of the show where we see Eleven attending school.

(208) Stranger Things 3 is the first season of the show where Will Byers appears in every episode.

(209) Hopper has the most screen time in season three.

(210) My Two Dads and Mad About You

(211) Bob Newby dies in The Mind Flayer.

(212) Priah Ferguson and Maya Hawke.

(213) Science.

(214) Their names often begin with the letter B. Benny, Barb, Bob, Billy, Bruce.

(215) Jamie Campbell Bower

(216) Ms. Kelly

(217) Grigori

(218) The special effects team found it tough to make Dustin's pet creature Dart seem cute and endearing because Demogorgons don't have eyes or visible features. In the end they had to make Dart's body language endearing to compensate.

(219) A nail spiked baseball bat.

(220) Hopper and Eleven.

(221) A part of Sleepy Hollow Farm is used for the exterior shots of Hopper's woodland cabin.

(222) Tommy

(223) Billy Hargrove

(224) Hopper took part in the Vietnam War.

(225) Stranger Things 4 is the first season not to feature Mr Clarke.

(226) 1983

(227) Hopper's sword is the same sword the hero had in Conan the Barbarian.

(228) Yuri

(229) Karen Wheeler is reading Tender is the Storm by Johanna Lindsey at the pool near the start of Stranger Things 3. The cover art depicts Billy Hargrove and Karen lookalikes as the lovers.

(230) Noah said he hates Will's signature bowl haircut!

(231) Aimee Mullins, who plays Terry Ives, competed in the

1996 Paralympics in Atlanta.

(232) This is obviously a reference to the fact that Sean Astin was in The Goonies.

(233) Until Dawn

(234) Lover's Lake

(235) A pizza dough freezer.

(236) Eleven is revealed to be a fan of Miami Vice in Stranger Things 3. Miami Vice was a police action drama show with Don Johnson that ran from 1984 to 1989.

(237) Needful Things and The Body

(238) Denis Villeneuve's 2013 movie Prisoners, a drama about a child that goes missing, was a big influence on season one of Stranger Things. The Duffer Brothers liked the idea of taking a drama story like this and giving it a big sci-fi twist.

(239) Trick or Treat, Freak. In this episode Steve and Nancy break up at the Halloween party.

(240) Skull Rock

(241) Among the games in the Palace Arcade you could have named are Asteroids, Galaga, Centipede, Dig Dug, Dragon's Lair, and Pac-Man.

(242) The Pollywog

(243) Sadie Sink nearly missed out on the part of Max Mayfield because she was deemed too tall compared to the rest of the kids. Luckily for her, the other young cast members had sufficient growth spurts.

(244) The arcade was a renovated laundromat located on 6500

Church Street in Douglasville, Georgia.

(245) Angela

(246) Debbie Nutty Bars, Bazooka bubble gum, Pez, Smarties, Pringles, Nilla Wafers, an apple, a banana, and some trail mix. Eleven ends up eating most of this food!

(247) Hazy Shade Of Winter

(248) The montage of Max and Eleven in the mall is backed by Madonna's Material Girl.

(249) The Dark Crystal

(250) Dustin wears Ghostbusters sneakers to the Snow Ball dance.

(251) Tom Cruise

(252) The scene very near the start of The Vanishing of Will Byers with the boys playing Dungeons & Dragons in Mike's basement was the very first scene ever filmed for Stranger Things.

(253) New Coke

(254) Dustin, Lucas, and Erica use Holly Wheeler's Lite-Brite to communicate with their friends over in the Upside Down.

(255) Joyce is working from home selling encyclopedias.

(256) Billy Hargrove

(257) Dustin complains that "these aren't real Nilla Wafers" when he tries the food at the funeral of Will. Nilla is a brand name owned by Nabisco that is most closely associated with its line of vanilla-flavored, wafer-style cookies.

(258) Nancy and Jonathan are fired from their positions at the Hawkins Post for their persistance in investigating Mrs Driscoll's rat problem.

(259) M&Ms.

(260) Dmitri Antonov

(261) The title sequence for Stranger Things is inspired by the title sequences for Bullit and The Terminator.

(262) The men at the Hawkins post mock Nancy by calling her "Nancy Drew" when she tries to investigate the rat mystery. Nancy Drew is fictional teenage amateur detective in an extended series of mystery books written by Carolyn Keene (a collective pseudonym, used by Edward Stratemeyer and, among many others, by his daughter Harriet S. Adams).

(263) Kali was originally going to be a male character named Roman.

(264) The Flea and the Acrobat is a reference to Mr Clarke's theory concerning alternate dimensions. Mr Clarke uses an analogy in Stranger Things to explain superstring theory and the multiverse to the boys when they ask him questions about other dimensions at the funeral of Will Byers. He tells them to imagine an acrobat on a rope. The acrobat can only go back and forwards. Then imagine a flea on the rope. The flea can go anywhere. It can even move around and come back to where it started. The flea had access to a dimension that the acrobat didn't.

(265) David Bowie

(266) Steve, Robin, Dustin, and Erica.

(267) Winona Ryder made her film debut in the cult 1986 teen drama/comedy Lucas with Corey Haim and Kerri Green.

(268) The arcade machines in Stranger Things 2 have modern flat plasma screens. This is definitely not period accurate to 1984.

(269) Brenner is shot by the army helicopter gunner in the desert as he tries to escape from the missile silo carrying Eleven.

(270) Linnea Berthelsen was born in India.

(271) $30 million per episode.

(272) Dustin says Suzie is hotter than Phoebe Cates.

(273) Coffee and contemplation.

(274) Mews

(275) Eleanor Gillespie

(276) Will coughs up a slug.

(277) Eddie borrows Max's Michael Myers mask from season two.

(278) There are no flights that would get Eleven there quick enough. She therefore has to go into the void to stop Vecna.

(279) In the season two episode Trick or Treat, Freak, a flashback shows us that Eleven escaped from the Upside Down version of Hawkins Middle School by dislodging rubble in the wall and crawling through a membrane which straddled the two dimensions.

(280) Tammy Thompson

(281) Joe Keery was working as a waiter to make ends meet when he was cast in Stranger Things.

(282) The Byers fridge in season three has an illustration depicting Bob Newby as a superhero.

(283) Dr Hatch

(284) Their bones begin to snap.

(285) His beloved guitar.

(286) The end of John Carpenter's Halloween when Dr Loomis shoots Michael Myers but the body disappears.

(287) Riverdale

(288) Sunburn.

(289) Shannon was working in a cinema when she was cast as Barb.

(290) Carter Burke

(291) It took two days to shoot the Snow Ball scenes.

(292) When It's Cold I'd Like to Die by Moby.

(293) The cabin belonged to Hopper's grandfather.

(294) Joyce and Hopper are the characters who went into the Upside Down to find Will.

(295) Texas

(296) Poltergeist

(297) Hopper's police jeep and uniform is based on Chief Brody (played of course by Roy Scheider) in Jaws.

(298) Cary Elwes is best known for his lead part in the cult 1987 fantasy film The Princess Bride.

(299) Natalia Dyer made her film debut in Hannah Montana: The Movie.

(300) The camera used by Jonathan Byers is a Pentax MX. This was a 35 mm single-lens reflex camera produced by Asahi Optical Co, later Pentax of Japan between 1976 and 1985.

(301) A 1976 Ford Pinto.

(302) Steve encounters a cut-out of Phoebe Cates from Fast Times at Ridgemont High at the video store.

(303) Gaten has a condition called cleidocranial dysplasia - a rare disorder that affects the growth of bones and teeth. Gaten's cleidocranial dysplasia was written into his character Dustin Henderson in Stranger Things. Gaten has campaigned to raise awareness of cleidocranial dysplasia. Gaten says that many sufferers have worse cases of the condition than he does.

(304) This is a line Maya Hawke's father Ethan Hawke said in the film Gattaca.

(305) Lonnie Byers

(306) Scrambled eggs.

(307) Firestarter. Firestarter is about a little girl named Charlie with pyrokinetic abilities which she gained from her parents taking a hallucinogenic known as 'Lot 6' as part of experiments when they were in college. A secret government agency known as 'The Shop' wants to use Charlie as a weapon. Stranger Things also borrows the idea of nosebleeds following the use of these extraordinary powers and the concept of a child's powers being weaponised for the military. When Drew Barrymore as Charlie is the subject of experiments in the film version she wears brain sensors - just like Eleven does when she's working for Dr Brenner in the Hawkins Lab.

(308) This is a reference to the loser's club in Stephen King's

It.

(309) Mike Wheeler wears Puma sneakers in the first season of Stranger Things.

(310) The Monster

(311) Polaroid cameras were a novelty in the eighties because you didn't have to take your photographs away to be developed. An instant photograph simply rolled out of the camera.

(312) The subtext is clearly the fact that Stranger Things only had eight episodes.

(313) The first ever scene is the scientist in the lab being chased (and caught) by an unseen monster when he reaches the elevator.

(314) Wonder Woman and Green Lantern.

(315) Holly Wheeler

(316) Stranger Things 4. Hopper has fewer lines in season four than any other season.

(317) Spring Break

(318) Hopper leaves some waffles in a box in the hope that Eleven is still alive and will find them.

(319) Lucas Conley

(320) Scream

(321) Mr Clarke was originally going to be based on Indiana Jones. He was going to be young and handsome and a main character in the show involved in all the danger and intrigue.

(322) The Monster

(323) Mike picks up a small trophy. This obviously wouldn't have been much use in fighting off DemoDogs!

(324) Stranger Things 4

(325) The Duffer Brothers said the character they had the most in common with when they were boys was Mike Wheeler.

(326) Stranger Things 4

(327) The Mall Rats

(328) MADMAX

(329) Loch Nora

(330) It was Millie Bobby Brown's idea for Mike and Eleven to kiss at the Snow Ball.

(331) Keith wants a date with Mike's sister Nancy. There is zero chance of this happening though!

(332) Max has a crush on Ralph Macchio - star of The Karate Kid.

(333) 2016

(334) Dustin wants to know how one would construct a sensory deprivation tank (so that Eleven can try and contact Will Byers).

(335) True. Millie Bobby Brown's hair is naturally curly if left to its own devices.

(336) James Dante

(337) The Griswolds are a fictional family who featured in the

1983 hit comedy film National Lampoon's Vacation. Chevy Chase played the head of the family, the accident prone Clark Griswold. There were numerous sequels.

(338) Jason is torn in half by a molten lava dimensional rip.

(339) Nancy is the first to dive in after Steve.

(340) Finn was the lead singer for a Vancouver band named Calpurnia from 2017 to 2019. Finn is now in a band called The Aubreys which consists of him and his former Calpurnia colleague Malcom Craig.

(341) Millie said she watched the Disney channel a lot to learn an American accent.

(342) The Massacre at Hawkins Lab

(343) The Upside Down and The Gate are both tied for the top spot.

(344) The 1985 film Witness when Lucas Haas points to Danny Glover's picture in the police station.

(345) Sixty pounds.

(346) Millie chose The Bathtub.

(347) The Monsters Are Due On Maple Street. In the episode, the residents of a usually peaceful and pleasant street descend into paranoia and witch hunts after a series of strange events which they suspect might involve aliens.

(348) Netflix wanted a clip of the van flip from the bike chase sequence in The Bathtub in the trailer.

(349) Because this was the first toy Mike showed Eleven when she lived in his basement.

(350) A train.

(351) Karen Wheeler

(352) Quantum of Solace

(353) Joe Chrest

(354) Bob's death in Stranger Things 2 is a homage to the gruesome death of Robert Shaw (as the shark hunter Quint) in Jaws.

(355) Noah Schnapp

(356) Patrick

(357) Cara Buono

(358) Finn said he liked Trick or Treat, Freak the most.

(359) Appropriately enough, Millie was eleven years old.

(360) This is a reference to Indy's sidekick Short Round being too small to reach the pedals of a car he drives in Indiana Jones and the Temple of Doom.

(361) Mike Wheeler has a calculator watch in season one. An Alpha Calc Chrono.

(362) Stranger Things 4

(363) The Soviet doctor who tortures Steve is named Dr Zharkov. Dr Zarkov is a character in Flash Gordon.

(364) Finn said he was more scared of Pennywise the Clown than the Demogorgon.

(365) Dr Owens wants to allow Eleven to leave the underground base and go to Hawkins to help her friends. Dr

Brenner, on the other hand, is adamant that Eleven should not leave until such time as he believes she is ready.

(366) Kate Bush

(367) Spiders.

(368) Holly, Jolly

(369) All My Children

(370) Jenn Woo

(371) Mileven

(372) Jennifer Hayes

(373) Steve being outflanked at the junkyard by DemoDogs evokes Bob Peck's gamekeeper outflanked by velociraptors in Jurassic Park.

(374) A stupid person or annoying person. If someone was getting on your nerves you might say - You are SUCH a mouthbreather.

(375) Peyton Wich played Troy.

(376) This is Suzie's price for telling Dustin the Planck's constant numbers needed for the mission in the Soviet base.

(377) A pollywog is a larval frog or toad, polliwog, or tadpole.

(378) Mr Clarke is at home listening to My Bologna by Weird Al Yankovic when he is visited by Joyce in season three. This song is a spoof of My Sharona by The Knack.

(379) Baskin-Robbins

(380) Samwise Gamgee

(381) 50/50. In future seasons though digital effects would become more dominant.

(382) Season three. Eleven seemed to blank Max at the end of season two when they first met.

(383) The first sensory deprivation tank (or chamber) was invented by John C. Lilly in 1954.

(384) Jo March in Little Women.

(385) Sesame Street

(386) Mark Steger was the man inside the Demogorgon suit in season one.

(387) False. The parents of Lucas were seen briefly during Will's funeral in season one.

(388) Levy is the coroner in the season one episode The Body.

(389) Kali's gang in season two are loosely inspired by the gang in the 1979 Walter Hill film The Warriors.

(390) Dustin Henderson

(391) Dr Brenner

(392) Winnie Kline

(393) Jason Hervey later became fairly well known for his role as Wayne Arnold in the comedy drama series The Wonder Years.

(394) Eleven freezes Troy and makes him pee his pants.

(395) A 1993 X-Files episode called Eve. The story has Mulder and Scully discovering a secret government project that involves children. The children are numbered - with the main

kids for the episode named Eve 9 and Eve 10.

(396) Froffles

(397) O'Bannon is a reference to Dan O'Bannon, who wrote the first draft of Ridley Scott's Alien and directed 1985's Return of the Living Dead.

(398) Altered States. The story is based on real life experiments by physician, neuroscientist, psychoanalyst, psychonaut, and philosopher Dr John Cunningham Lilly. Lilly invented the sensory deprivation tank.

(399) Karate.

(400) This game is fictitious and based on the fact that one of the production crew had a music band called Space Knife.

(401) The song that plays during Will's funeral in season one is Elegia by New Order.

(402) The Peterbilt truck that features in the season two episode Dig Dug is an in-joke regarding the episode's director Andrew Stanton's Pixar film Cars.

(403) Mike puts syrup on his eggs.

(404) The Snow Ball dance.

(405) Stranger Things 4

(406) Millie said she only had 25 followers on Instagram before Stranger Things. She now has 58 million.

(407) This is a line that Roy Scheider (as Chief Brody) says in Jaws.

(408) Noah was away at summer camp when he got the news he'd won the part of Will Byers.

(409) The scar on Eleven's shin is from where the Flayer parasite was removed in season three.

(410) The TRC-214 walkie-talkies the boys use in Stranger Things had a radius of one mile.

(411) The Wizard of Oz

(412) Wake Me Up Before You Go-Go by Wham!

(413) The wristband was a hairband which belonged to Hopper's late daughter Sara.

(414) Will Byers seems to give his Dungeons & Dragons stuff to Erica at the end of Stranger Things 3.

(415) False. The Goonies was released about four weeks before Stranger Things 3 takes place but doesn't feature at the Starcourt Mall cinema.

(416) Vecna's Curse

(417) Noah Schnapp. It was only from season two that Noah was based in Atlanta like the rest of the cast. Noah obviously had fewer scenes to shoot on season one because Will Byers is trapped in the Upside Down and not seen that much.

(418) One. Dr Owens merely makes a brief appearance in the season three finale.

(419) Peanut butter

(420) France

(421) Steve has a BMW.

(422) The term 'ham' means 'amateur' - as in amateur radio.

(423) A group of flying bats.

(424) 1980

(425) The pitch booklet said - Mike is the Elliot of our show, Eleven is our E.T.

(426) A tragic car accident.

(427) Hopper was involved in the preparation of the chemical Agent Orange when he served in Vietnam. He believes this might be why his daughter got cancer.

(428) The tornado sequence in The Wizard of Oz.

(429) Dacre got stuck to a table during lunch because he'd had so much glue applied to him.

(430) Natalia Dyer and Millie Bobby Brown.

(431) Scream

(432) New York State

(433) In the pilot script, Benny's Burgers was a Fish and Chip themed diner.

(434) David Harbour said the worst thing was that the Hazmat suit took half an hour to take off before you could use the bathroom!

(435) Eleven's age is not stated but it is suggested she is twelve in season one because that's how long Terry Ives has been looking for her.

(436) Noah Schnapp

(437) Hopper takes a bottle of vodka.

(438) They seem to think Eddie Munson is a Devil worshipping serial killer.

(439) Lucas has joined the basketball team because he doesn't want to be a D&D 'nerd' anymore.

(440) Two.

(441) Les Misérables

(442) The Tonight Show

(443) Millie Bobby Brown

(444) A shrine to Barb was created by fans at the 2017 Comic Con.

(445) Eleven wants to go out trick or treating but Hopper insists she must stay hidden.

(446) The Duffer Brothers were wary of doing the possession storyline with Will Byers since this sort of horror plot had been done so many times before.

(447) Ratt performing Round and Round from the album Out of the Cellar.

(448) Will has painted his friends battling a dragon.

(449) Bob is the only one who knows BASIC computer code.

(450) E.T. the Extra-Terrestrial

(451) Knight Rider. The show had David Hasselhoff as an enigmatic crime fighter equipped with a futuristic car that has artificial intelligence.

(452) This is a meta joke based on the fact that in the cult 1982 film Diner, Paul Reiser played a character who was always asking people if he could have the last half of their sandwich.

(453) Suzie Bingham

(454) Suzie's house looks like the one from Home Alone.

(455) "A game where you toss balls into laundry baskets."

(456) Eleven seems to be wearing a ring in season four.

(457) Kate Capshaw as Willie Scott in Indiana Jones and the Temple of Doom.

(458) Eleven is annoyed because Mike never puts 'love' at the end of them.

(459) Eleven comes to suspect that Brenner wanted her to try and find Henry Creel in the void.

(460) False. Millie said she doesn't mind Eggos but never really eats them because she isn't a breakfast person.

(461) Argyle

(462) True.

(463) As punishment for Suzie helping Dustin cheat on his grades through computer hacking.

(464) The Lost Sister

(465) Two. MADMAX and The Lost Sister.

(466) True.

(467) David Harbour

(468) Season three

(469) Hopper wants Joyce to see for herself that the lab is now closed and derelict.

(470) Eddie

(471) Burger and fries.

(472) 8,000 calories

(473) This is a very obvious tribute to Close Encounters of the Third Kind.

(474) The opening of Starcourt Mall has clearly made it difficult for traditional shops to compete.

(475) We see a parched Hopper chug down some Jolt Cola in the gas station after his escapades on the road.

(476) The Thing

(477) The Bathtub

(478) Gumby is a clay animation franchise, centred on a green clay humanoid character created and modeled by Art Clokey. The character has been the subject of two television series, a feature-length film and other media.

(479) Two. Levy always directs the third and fourth episodes.

(480) Fallout 3

(481) Because the military and Sullivan are still after her.

(482) The Fortress of Solitude is Superman's secret base and ice glazed retreat in DC Comics.

(483) This piece of music was written by Philip Glass for the 1982 time lapse non-linear film Koyaanisqatsi. The music also featured in the film adaption of Alan Moore's Watchmen comic.

(484) Shorts. They had to wear shorts a lot because season three is set in the summer.

(485) A scene in the 1983 adaptation of Stephen King's The Dead Zone in which Christopher Walken and Tom Skerritt find a bloodied body in a bathtub.

(486) False. Joe Keery didn't find it amusing when he learned that Steve would be in this costume for practically the whole season. Keery said that when he got the season three scripts he kept reading on, expecting a costume change for Steve, but it never arrived until the end of the finale when Steve visits Keith's video store with Robin.

(487) The Soviets are using a machine to try and access the Upside Down. This experiment does not work.

(488) John McClane near the end of Die Hard.

(489) Vecna

(490) The Sauna Test

(491) Predator

(492) Winona Ryder

(493) Volcanic eruptions and lightning storms.

(494) Mike needs coins for the video game arcade.

(495) Dungeons & Dragons

(496) Kali

(497) Predators

(498) True. Jamie Campbell Bower said he had to break character and give Millie a comforting hug at one point.

(499) Finn Wolfhard

(500) Joe Keery hurt his back in the junkyard sequence in season two because he had to do so many takes of him jumping into the bus.

(501) Eleven breaks his arm.

(502) A new camera to replace the one he smashed.

(503) Stand By Me

(504) Stranger Things 3

(505) By scrubbing off graffitti he has written about Nancy.

(506) Charlize Theron in Mad Max: Fury Road.

(507) Susan Shalhoub Larkin is the sister of Monk and Galaxy Quest actor Tony Shalhoub.

(508) The reunion of Mike and Eleven was originally going to occur at the Snow Ball dance but the Duffers decided to have them meet again at the end of the penultimate episode instead.

(509) The Duffers communicated with Millie through a radio in her ear.

(510) Lucas

(511) A furniture store.

(512) Charlie Brown

(513) Watermelon

(514) Paul Reiser was fired from Bachelor Party a week into production and replaced by Tom Hanks.

(515) Twenty tons of ice were needed to make Georgia look like Hawkins in winter.

(516) Millie Bobby Brown

(517) Steve's red bandana in the tunnels for Stranger Things 2 is a tribute to the red bandana worn by Josh Brolin in The Goonies.

(518) Finn Wolfhard. Finn said the gears were messed up and the bike was heavy.

(519) Nancy Wheeler

(520) Bob Newby

(521) Molotov cocktails.

(522) Jonathan, Will, Mike, and Argyle.

(523) Eleven

(524) By use of fire through a flaming torch fashioned with a bandage and lit alcohol.

(525) You could have picked any three out of The Empire Strikes Back, Godfather Part II, Terminator 2, Aliens, Toy Story 2, Evil Dead 2, and Indiana Jones and the Temple of Doom.

(526) That was obviously Hopper.

(527) The Duffer Brothers showed Noah Schnapp's mother the realistic Will Byers morgue dummy for a joke.

(528) 162 calories.

(529) The Duffers were initially going to have Dustin and Suzie sing the Ent song from Lord Of The Rings but they axed this plan when they heard that Amazon were making a television show based on Lord of the Rings.

(530) Time After Time

(531) Blueberry

(532) Dustin's mother is clearly a Democrat as she has a Walter Mondale placard on her lawn.

(533) Three.

(534) During the construction of the home-made sensory deprivation water tank in The Bathtub.

(535) Millie chose the Byers' dog Chester!

(536) It Follows

(537) 'We are not in Hawkins anymore'

(538) The Duffers said this was David Harbour's idea.

(539) She trickled some of her blood into the swimming pool.

(540) There is no rain in the tapes.

(541) Promise.

(542) The Bathtub

(543) True

(544) You could have chosen, among others, Flashdance, Rocky, Animal House, The Karate Kid, Footloose, and Risky Business.

(545) As a tribute to Indiana Jones.

(546) A movement that sprung up in fandom concerning the early demise of Barb Holland. The main driver of the movement was the observation that - Nancy aside - no one in

the show seemed to notice or care much that Barb had suddenly vanished without trace.

(547) Tennessee

(548) Season one. Randall Havens as Mr Clarke has 53 lines in season one.

(549) David Harbour. Harbour said didn't encounter a single poster or ad promoting the show and was worried that Netflix might have 'buried' Stranger Things. Harbour was fearful that no one would even notice the show when it became available to stream. His fears proved unfounded

(550) Dustin adopting a strange pet.

(551) Maine is the home of Stephen King.

(552) Television static represented the supernatural in Poltergeist.

(553) "Bad place."

(554) Ford

(555) A helicopter.

(556) The New Mutants

(557) Dustin is clearly dressed as an Ewok.

(558) Police Academy 3: Back in Training

(559) Max

(560) 1984

(561) Agent Ellen Stinson

(562) Winona Ryder

(563) Steve and Nancy

(564) Bitching!

(565) A tutor and a classroom.

(566) Code-red.

(567) Finn Wolfhard

(568) Millie said she had some mint tic-tacs.

(569) Shannon said she had wanted to keep Barb's spectacles.

(570) They watch some golf.

(571) Angel

(572) Jonathan Byers

(573) Winona Ryder

(574) Noah Schnap and Millie Bobby Brown.

(575) Meatloaf, mashed potato and green beans.

(576) Priah Ferguson as Erica Sinclair.

(577) Joe Keery

(578) Henry Cavill. Cavill was in Enola Homes.

(579) Glennellen Anderson auditioned to play Barb.

(580) The look of the Upside Down.

(581) False. Charlie says he never watches horror movies.

(582) Drones. The media were trying to capture footage and photographs.

(583) Pac-Man

(584) Grigori

(585) The Bathtub

(586) Gaten Matarazzo. Gaten prefers his hair shorter than Dustin Henderson.

(587) Dustin Henderson

(588) Gaten Matarazzo

(589) Finn as Mike Wheeler has seventy lines in The Weirdo on Maple Street. This is the most lines any character has in any episode of season one of Stranger Things.

(590) He had to do the canteen monologue which introduces us to Eddie.

(591) The Guest

(592) Eisenhower

(593) Mr Clarke

(594) Two.

(595) Mike Wheeler

(596) No! Fruit on a pizza is a definite no-no for Mike Wheeler.

(597) The Body

(598) She uses her powers to skew their compass readings and

send them off the trail.

(599) "If anyone asks I've left the country!"

(600) Because he knows this would harm Will Byers given that Will is connected to the Upside Down.

(601) Suzie

(602) The lab room leading into the rift in Stranger Things 2

(603) Eleven finds a box marked Vietnam.

(604) Funshine is a member of Kali's gang in season two.

(605) 'Breathe' was Terry giving birth. 'Sunflower' was a vase she awoke to. 'Rainbow' was a child's room she found in the Hawkins Lab. 'Three to the right, four to the left' was the safe combination she used to get a gun so that she could go to the lab and get Jane back. '450' was the voltage of the treatment Brenner gave her to ensure her silence.

(606) Nancy says they are going 'Monster hunting".

(607) Yes. Eleven seems to enjoy Argyle's pineapple laden pizza in the season four finale.

(608) The scene in Saving Private Ryan where Tom Hanks fires a futile shot at a tank just as the tank is about to be bombed by an aircraft.

(609) Once Upon a Time in Hollywood

(610) Dr Brenner

(611) Christmas lights.

(612) Finn Wolfhard

(613) The boys refer to proton packs on their Ghostbusters costumes in Stranger Things 2. This is a mistake because that term was only used in the 1989 sequel. The correct term in 1984 would have been positron colliders.

(614) Gaten said he was banned from sending his brother any texts about the show. The cast members have to make sure no spoilers leak beyond the set.

(615) David Harbour

(616) Predator

(617) The Flea and the Acrobat

(618) Holly, Jolly

(619) The Bathtub

(620) Karen Wheeler

(621) Andrey Ivchenko

(622) Lucas and Max.

(623) A snowmobile.

(624) Red Ranger (Jason Scott)

(625) True.

(626) A physical constant that is the quantum of electromagnetic action.

(627) Season four

(628) They would go to theme parks together.

(629) Friends don't lie.

(630) The film is called Network.

(631) Stranger Things 4

(632) Dacre Montgomery took a couple of Billy's tank tops home with him.

(633) Finn Wolfhard said his favourite scene in the third season was when Dustin and Suzie sing the Neverending Story song.

(634) Dragon magazine. This was a magazine for enthusiasts of Dungeons & Dragons.

(635) Mayor Kline

(636) You could have chosen from The Stuff, Lifeforce, Fletch, Return to Oz, DARYL, Cocoon, Weird Science, Back to the Future, Day of the Dead, and The Black Cauldron.

(637) Sam Raimi's Darkman

(638) True.

(639) The Catcher in the Rye

(640) Jack Nicholson driving his family to the hotel in The Shining.

(641) Jonathan worked in a cinema.

(642) The Plane of Shadows. The Plane of Shadows is a dimension that exists alongside our own reality.

(643) Sadie Sink

(644) Beverly Hills Cop

(645) Neil Hargrove

(646) Intruders

(647) Voldemort

(648) You can hear a snatch of music from the Dungeons & Dragons cartoon in season three when Hopper and Joyce are at the fair.

(649) Dustin Henderson

(650) Dr Owens is introduced just as Carter Burke was in Aliens. Both are by a hospital bed and asking the patient (Ellen Ripley and Will Byers respectively) to trust them.

(651) Fleabag

(652) Kenny Rogers

(653) Because each of the actors/characters had to have three back up bikes (for stunts and in case of accidents) and it was impossible to find that many vintage identical bikes from the eighties.

(654) Bob accidentally knocks over a broom.

(655) Murray seems to believe there is a Soviet conspiracy afoot.

(656) Barb cut her finger trying to shotgun some beer.

(657) The famous World War 2 photograph where six United States Marines raised the flag atop Mount Suribachi at the Battle of Iwo Jima.

(658) Hellboy

(659) Will Byers would have been eight in 1979 but in 1979 Crayola didn't sell 120-crayon boxes.

(660) Gaten Matarazzo

(661) Alec Utgoff

(662) Three days.

(663) Millie said she was more scared of ghosts.

(664) No. Many famous companies are visible but none of them pay to be in the show.

(665) Sliced turkey with gravy, peas and mashed potatoes.

(666) Noah Schnapp

(667) Karen has a change of heart after looking at Ted and Holly asleep in a chair.

(668) Dr Owens

(669) Finn Wolfhard

(670) The girls admiring Billy's posterior are sitting against a Mustang.

(671) Stranger Things 3 is clearly 'peak neon' when it comes to Stranger Things.

(672) Dacre said he drew on his own experiences of bullying.

(673) Mike was supposed to wear an E.T watch but they couldn't get the rights.

(674) You Don't Mess Around with Jim by Jim Croce

(675) Mike Wheeler

(676) A shark.

(677) Shannon was actually in a cinema watching a film when she got the good news.

(678) Bob Newby's death was originally going to be more blood drenched but they decided to soften this somewhat.

(679) On the first take of the stunt where Eleven flips the van over the bicycles, one of the explosives failed and the van ended up destroying an expensive camera.

(680) Linnea Berthelsen. She said she'd never seen Stranger Things when she was asked to audition for it and so stayed up until 4 in the morning binge watching the first season.

(681) Princess Leia

(682) Nancy Wheeler is the name of a character in Judy Blume's young fiction novel Are You There God? It's Me, Margaret.

(683) Cake frosting.

(684) Eleven

(685) The Massacre at Hawkins Lab

(686) Jason Carver

(687) Billy's dad evidently left her mother after Billy died so finances are tight.

(688) Erica

(689) Steve finds the infamous Christmas lights from season one while he is rummaging around.

(690) Levon Thurman-Hawke - younger brother of Maya Hawke - has a cameo in the video store.

(691) Charlie Heaton

(692) Monsters Inc

(693) Dustin Henderson

(694) Steve and Billy

(695) Carroll is watching Punky Brewster. Punky Brewster was a sitcom for younger viewers about an orphan girl adopted by a cranky but kind hearted man.

(696) View-Master is the trademark name of a line of special-format stereoscopes and corresponding View-Master "reels", which are thin cardboard disks containing seven stereoscopic 3-D pairs of small colour photographs on film. In the 1980s, many kids had View-Masters and they often had film tie-in slides to view.

(697) "Holy s***, what happened to you?"

(698) Paul Reiser and Matthew Modine starred together in the 1995 film Bye Bye Love.

(699) Hockey gear.

(700) Chevy vans.

(701) The Duffers said the boys kept breaking wind.

(702) Noah Schnapp and Winona Ryder unsuccessfully lobbied the Duffers to not kill off Bob Newby in Stranger Things 2 because they loved working with Sean Astin so much.

(703) The name of the character Jonathan Byers is seen as a possible tribute/reference to John Fitzgerald Byers, one of the 'Lone Gunmen' in The X-Files.

(704) Volkswagen

(705) True.

(706) Joe Chrest, who plays Ted Wheeler.

(707) Millie Bobby Brown famously did not enjoy being kissed by Finn Wolfhard when Mike kisses Eleven in the first season finale. When the director yelled "cut!", she declared that "kissing sucks!" - much to the amusement of Wolfhard and the crew.

(708) Dustin has a certificate of Anti-Paranormal Proficiency on his wall from the Ghostbusters official fan club in Stranger Things 2.

(709) Zombie Boy

(710) Back to the Future - where the mailbox at Peabody's farm is destroyed when Otis Peabody shoots at the DeLorean.

(711) Baldo the clown.

(712) Nancy is in the same pose as Adrienne Barbeau shooting at the Duke's car in John Carpenter's Escape from New York.

(713) Duran Duran's Hungry Like the Wolf.

(714) Millie Bobby Brown

(715) Joe Dante's The Howling

(716) Joyce Byers

(717) Randall Flagg (the villain in Stephen King's book The Stand), Rob Lowe in the 80s Brat Pack drama St Elmo's Fire, and Jason Patric in 1987 vampire film The Lost Boys.

(718) A Nightmare On Elm Street

(719) Hopper line was said by Jeff Goldblum in Jurassic Park.

(720) Eleven's hairstyle.

(721) Nancy Wheeler

(722) Matty Cardarople, who plays the Cheeto loving Keith, is the tallest Stranger Things cast member at 6'4. He only just edges out Matthew Modine - who is 6'3.

(723) True. Jake Busey said he did so many auditions during pilot season they all became a blur in the end.

(724) It took a week to shoot the scenes in The Sauna Test where the kids trap Billy in the sauna.

(725) 1990

(726) Hopper

(727) The Hunt for Red October

(728) Brimborn Steel Works

(729) Yes. Brenner very briefly appears in a vision Eleven has in The Lost Sister.

(730) We don't actually know because it is never mentioned in season three. One of the Stranger Things comics states that the creature turned into sludge and dissolved.

(731) True.

(732) This is a reference to the 1979 coming of age drama Breaking Away. Breaking Away, which features a cycling obsessed character who pretends to be Italian, is set in Indiana - just like Stranger Things.

(733) Brenner has a scar from where he was attacked by the Demogorgon in season one.

(734) Kali escaped from the lab before that fateful day so she wasn't there.

(735) The day Will Byers went missing.

(736) Four.

(737) Both are British.

(738) Katinka

(739) A Russian doll.

(740) The Hawkins Post

(741) The Flea and the Acrobat

(742) November

(743) Sean Astin. Astin auditioned for the part of Gordie played by Wil Wheaton.

(744) Because the bully Troy was threatening Dustin with a knife and ordered him to do it.

(745) A music mix tape.

(746) Killer Klowns from Outer Space

(747) Nike

(748) The Spy and Dear Billy

(749) Sadie Sink

(750) Pennhurst Mental Hospital

(751) An ice cream scooper.

(752) This is a homage to a shot in David Fincher's Alien 3 where the Xenomorph does the same thing to Sigourney Weaver's Ripley.

(753) A Benny's Burgers t-shirt.

(754) When she closes the dimensional Gate in the season two finale.

(755) The Monster and the Superhero

(756) It's safe to say that not noticing the Red Army are active in an Indiana mall and trying to drill into the Upside Down is probably fair grounds for dismissal!

(757) Millie Bobby Brown only has forty-two lines as Eleven in the whole of season one.

(758) The Duffers say that Dr Brenner was probably the hardest character to write in Stranger Things because he is so self-contained and doesn't say very much.

(759) John Reynolds, who plays Officer Callahan, says he is one of the few cast members who never seems to get recognised by anyone.

(760) True. Millie said it made her head itch.

(761) Cara Buono wore waterproof mascara so that her eye make-up wouldn't smudge in the scene where Karen climbs out of the pool to talk to Billy.

(762) Will Byers has a Nelsonic Q-bert game watch in Stranger Things 3.

(763) Stalker. The film revolves around an expedition to a mysterious restricted area known as the Zone.

(764) This line is a reference to the 1992 Robert Redford film

Sneakers, which has the line - "It's fascinating what 50 bucks will get you at the county recorder's office. Playtronics Corporate Headquarters, the complete blueprints."

(765) A Volvo.

(766) The Duffers said they felt some guilt at killing Barb off so quickly because it was Shannon Purser's first acting job and she was so nice to work with.

(767) The Spy

(768) Stacey is one of the girls who snubs Dustin when he is looking for someone to dance with at the Snow Ball in season two. Stacey is played by Sydney Bullock. In season two, Stacey sneers at Eleven and Max having fun at the mall. Eleven extracts an amusing revenge by making Stacey's Orange Julius drink explode.

(769) Steve picks Animal House, Back to the Future, and the Star Wars film with teddy bears (by which he obviously means Return of the Jedi).

(770) Summer of Night. The story is set in a small town in the 1960s and revolves around a small gang of boys who must battle an evil which awakens.

(771) The scenes where the Flayer infested Will Byers is tied to a chair are inspired by the sequence in The Thing where the men at the base are restrained and have their blood tested to see which one of them might be the alien.

(772) A bully named Troy is mentioned in The Goonies.

(773) The 1994 James Cameron film True Lies.

(774) Because he gave Brenner the location of Eleven in return for access to the Upside Down and a shot at saving Will Byers.

(775) Steve Harrington

(776) When she slams a door shut with her mind in The Weirdo on Maple Street in protest at the plan to inform Mike's mother of her presence.

(777) David Harbour, Noah Schnapp, and Dacre Montgomery all had to wear hairpieces in season two.

(778) Will the Wise

(779) David Harbour shaved his head for Stranger Things 4 to avoid any resemblance with his character from Black Widow - who also spends time in a Russian prison.

(780) Two.

(781) Way back in the season one second episode The Weirdo on Maple Street. After smuggling Eleven into Mike's basement, Lucas suggests (rather improbably) that she might be an escaped lunatic from Pennhurst!

(782) He played Gellert Grindelwald in Harry Potter and the Deathly Hallows – Part 1 and Fantastic Beasts: The Crimes of Grindelwald

(783) Michael Biehn's Hicks says the same thing in Aliens.

(784) Alexei is a Soviet scientist.

(785) Morten Harket. Morten Harket was the lead singer of A-ha.

(786) He-Man and the Masters of the Universe

(787) Mike Wheeler

(788) Charlie Heaton, who is from Yorkshire in England, had an absolutely torturous time on the show trying to say the

name Nancy in an American accent so in the end they simply decided to dub him whenever this name cropped up in relation to his character (and it obviously cropped up a LOT given that his character Jonathan is Nancy's boyfriend in most of the show).

(789) Trapper Keeper

(790) Twice.

(791) False. The Duffers and Shawn Levy said that they never seriously considered bringing Barb back.

(792) Tostito chips and salsa.

(793) Grigori

(794) The song was famously used in Kubrick's Dr Strangelove.

(795) Richard Pryor as Gus Gorman in Superman III struggling with a similar predicament.

(796) Bo Derek

(797) Whipped cream, Reese's Pieces, Hershey's Kisses, and jelly beans.

(798) Eleven uses her powers to turn off a droning fan that is irritating her.

(799) Joyce moves out of Hawkins with her family at the end of season three.

(800) The Hellfire Club

(801) In reality the Department of Energy (DOE) is a Cabinet-level department of the United States Government concerned with the United States' policies regarding energy and safety in

handling nuclear material.

(802) True. His only condition on agreeing to do this was that he got the first slice of wedding cake.

(803) The Duffers didn't have a name for Dr Owens at first so in the early Stranger Things 2 script drafts they called him Dr Paul Reiser in tribute to Carter Burke (who was obviously played by Reiser) from James Cameron's 1986 film Aliens.

(804) Dustin Henderson

(805) Finn Wolfhard wasn't on the set that day and so Millie had to react to nothing.

(806) Lonnie goes to see Joyce to lend support but we eventually learn that his main motivation seems to be making a claim against the quarry where Will 'died' so that he can reap a financial windfall.

(807) Hopper

(808) True. The place where Gaten worked as a food runner during the hiatus in production on Stranger Things 4 was Bird & Betty's on Long Beach Island.

(809) Matt Duffer. Ross Duffer initially didn't like Stranger Things as the title but came around to it in the end.

(810) Murray Bauman

(811) The scene in the 1994 film The Shawshank Redemption where the warden finds the tunnel in the wall that Andy Dufresne had dug to escape.

(812) Synth

(813) Eleven

(814) V

(815) The portal is on the ceiling of Eddie's trailer.

(816) Dimensional portals.

(817) The Satanic Panic was a campaign against Dungeons & Dragons by various religious and parent groups. They believed the game was dangerous and encouraged a belief in black magic and the occult.

(818) Ten.

(819) Three years.

(820) The film director Ridley Scott and science fiction author Arthur C. Clarke.

(821) Two. The heads are named Aemeul and Hethradiah.

(822) Other titles the Duffers considered were Indigo, The Rift, The Nether, Sentinel, Flickers, The Keep, The Tesseract, and Wormhole.

(823) Millie Bobby Brown

(824) Noah Schnapp

(825) In the basement of her parents home.

(826) Dan Aykroyd and Ivan Reitman (Aykroyd and Reitman held the rights to Ghostbusters).

(827) The hive sequence in James Cameron's Aliens where the Colonial Marines are attacked by the aliens.

(828) David Harbour, Finn Wolfhard, and Millie Bobby Brown have all said this.

(829) Bridge of Spies. Noah played the son of Tom Hanks.

(830) Twenty-three

(831) Project MKUltra was a top secret CIA funded experiment into mind control that made use of the mind-altering drug LSD. The MKUltra experiments included attempts at remote viewing and extrasensory perception. Project MKUltra ended in 1973 and only became public knowledge after the experiment was terminated.

(832) Hidden. Hidden was made in 2012 but sat on the shelf for four years.

(833) The scene where Nancy is reduced to tears in the Holland bathroom.

(834) Mike Wheeler was supposed to carry the exhausted Eleven into the classroom. However, Finn Wolfhard found it too difficult to carry Millie Bobby Brown so Gaten Matarazzo (as Dustin obviously) did it instead.

(835) The Hawkins library.

(836) Gaten Matarazzo

(837) Mrs Driscoll

(838) When Will is rescued from the Upside Down in the season one finale, Hopper and Joyce seem to be at (the dark mirror version of) the Hawkins Library.

(839) New Coke. "The original is a classic, no question about it. But the remake - sweeter, bolder, better."

(840) The Farrah Fawcett hairspray from Stranger Things 2.

(841) Steve Harrington

(842) One. Kali has yet to return after her appearances in season two.

(843) Stranger Things 4. This was due to pandemic halting shooting and giving the Duffers several more months to write.

(844) Gordon Ramsay's Hell's Kitchen

(845) The 1995 Kevin Smith comedy film Mallrats.

(846) Dear Billy

(847) The Monster and the Superhero

(848) A camera date at the roller rink establishes that it is Will's birthday but there is no mention of this by anyone. The Duffers confessed that they simply forgot the date of Will's birthday.

(849) Season three.

(850) Some sausage and pepperoni pizza.

(851) Heather the lifeguard's house in Stranger Things 3 is deliberately similar to Heather Langenkamp's house in Wes Craven's A Nightmare on Elm Street.

(852) The Duffers said they wanted to put the audience on their toes and feel like the characters in Hawkins were not safe.

(853) Grey's Anatomy

(854) Joe Keery, Finn Wolfhard, Charlie Heaton, and Gaten Matarazzo have been in bands.

(855) It closed because of a mould problem in the building.

(856) It appears to be an Atari gaming system.

(857) The periodic table contains some elements that hadn't been discovered yet in 1984.

(858) Carrie

(859) 1971

(860) Dungeons & Dragons was subject to legal action from the Tolkien estate for its similarities to Lord of the Rings and The Hobbit.

(861) Woody Woodpecker

(862) Joe Keery had to do the scene where Steve smashes Jonathan's camera.

(863) The corridor sequence at the start of the original Star Wars.

(864) Rambo: First Blood Part II

(865) According to Sadie Sink, it was Millie Bobby Brown who suggested this to the Duffers.

(866) Back at Hopper's cabin.

(867) The Hawkins Department of Energy building in Stranger Things is the former Georgia Mental Health Institute. This mental institution closed down years ago.

(868) Operation Child Endangerment!

(869) $4 + 2 + 2 = 8$

(870) The other children were killed by Ballard/Henry Creel in 1979.

(871) True.

(872) 'Dear Mike, I have gone to become a superhero again. From, El.'

(873) Dear Billy.

(874) Troy and James only appeared in season one.

(875) Pancakes

(876) In tribute to Kobe Bryant.

(877) Reebok

(878) To buy more time for Steve's gang by distracting the DemoBats. Eddie also still feels guilt because he ran away from Chrissy when Vecna struck.

(879) Reefer Rick's boat house.

(880) Microfiche is a flat piece of film containing microphotographs of the pages of a newspaper, catalogue, or other document.

(881) The BFG

(882) Winona Ryder

(883) Winona Ryder famously featured with Mr Mom star Michael Keaton in Tim Burton's Beetlejuice.

(884) They couldn't find a large enough tunnel in Atlanta for the car chase and so had to extend one with CGI.

(885) Joe and Dacre had to have some basketball practice.

(886) Cornelius

(887) Maya Hawke turned off her social media in case people didn't like her character Robin.

(888) The twins played the baby Eleven in the season two flashbacks set in the lab.

(889) Eden

(890) War Zone

(891) Cheers. Cheers is a classic 80s/90s sitcom set in a Boston bar where everyone knows your name.

(892) Noah Schnapp researched possessed people to prepare for Stranger Things 2.

(893) Five

(894) This scene is a homage to Gene Hackman doing a similar thing in the classic seventies Francis Ford Coppola film The Conversation.

(896) Dustin is wearing a Castroville Artichoke Festival t-shirt in the last two episodes of season one.

(897) Millie Bobby Brown was only told she would have to cut her long hair off for the part of Eleven after the final audition.

(898) None. The part was given straight to Gaten.

(899) The Invisibles

(900) Full Metal Jacket

(901) Max has a poster for the 1966 surf movie The Endless Summer in her room.

(902) The fight between Jonathan Steve in season one is a homage to the alleyway fistfight between Roddy Piper and David Keith in the John Carpenter movie They Live.

(903) Neutron Dance became famous when it was used on the

soundtrack to the hit 1984 Eddie Murphy film Beverly Hills Cop.

(904) E Pluribus Unum is Latin for "out of many, one." Sometimes it is translated more loosely as "one from many." E Pluribus Unum was once the motto of the United States of America and references the fact that a single nation was formed as the result of the thirteen smaller colonies joining together.

(905) The doomed scientist is called Shephard.

(906) Millie supports Liverpool.

(907) Max

(908) True. Benny was called Benny Henderson in the pilot script.

(909) None. The rats were all computer generated.

(910) Millie suffered from motion sickness.

(911) Beetlejuice. This is a little in-joke because Winona Ryder was in Beetlejuice.

(912) Hellraiser

(913) Sadie had to have some fake tan applied because Max is supposed to be from California.

(914) Lucas and Mike.

(915) The Freeling family home in Poltergeist.

(916) Caleb McLaughlin

(917) Millie Bobby Brown and Sadie Sink.

(918) Finn Wolfhard

(919) Some of John Harrison's music for George A Romero's Day of the Dead can be heard during the scenes between Steve and Robin. The specific piece of music is called Sarah Breaks Down.

(920) Lucas Sinclair

(921) False. Limahl said he had never even heard of Stranger Things until they used his Neverending Story song.

(922) Red Dawn

(923) Jason and his players hang out at the boarded up Benny's Burgers.

(924) The Duffer Brothers said that the 2011 JJ Abrams film Super 8 was an influence on Stranger Things. Super 8 is set in the late 1970s and has a gang of children investigating a strange mystery in their small town.

(925) My Little Pony

(926) Billy Hargrove and Dr Brenner.

(927) The Nina Project

(928) Stranger Things 3

(929) Every Breath You Take by The Police

(930) Millie said the waffles she had to eat in season one were not very fresh.

(931) The holster is for Steve's ice cream scooper.

(932) Millie said she lost her voice five times on season three because of all the screaming she had to do.

(933) Private School starred a young Matthew Modine.

(934) Noah had a headache during his audition and presumed he hadn't done very well.

(935) Martie Marie Blair was the body double for the younger version of Eleven we occasionally see in Stranger Things 4.

(936) The Montauk Project. The Montauk Project is a conspiracy theory that revolves around the decommissioned Montauk Air Force Station located at the east end of the Long Island peninsula. The conspiracy theories surrounding the defunct base include teleportation, time travel, super powered children, and contact with aliens.

(937) Robin uses the computer to see which movies people called Rick have rented. Through this she is able to deduce which one of them is Eddie's drug supplier.

(938) Canada

(939) False. Steve and Dustin were only put together on a whim when season two was deep into production.

(940) Brett Gelman had to take some Russian language lessons.

(941) Millie Bobby Brown says she used 'method' acting to play the scene at the end of Stranger Things 3 where Eleven reads the letter from Hopper. Millie only read Hopper's speech for the first time in the actual scene - thus making it more emotional.

(942) David Harbour also played an inmate in a Russian prison for the film Black Widow.

(943) True. However, Gabriella Pizzolo on the other hand, who plays Suzie, was already a big fan of the film.

(944) Noah said the scene he loves the most is when Eleven flips the van up in the air during the bike chase in season one.

(945) $40,000

(946) Ted Bundy is probably the most famous serial killer in American history. He executed by electric chair in 1989 for 30+ murders.

(947) Mayor Kline has a Mercedes-Benz.

(948) Malibu

(949) Godzilla: King of the Monsters

(950) Erica requests free ice cream for life!

(951) Die Hard

(952) Eleven hits Angela in the face with a roller skate.

(953) A 1985 Chrysler Lebaron Convertible.

(954) The school canteen.

(955) Paul Reiser is the richest member of the Stranger Things cast. He's said to be worth $75 million.

(956) Fraggle Rock. Fraggle Rock was a Jim Henson television show in the vein of The Muppets.

(957) Stranger Things 4. Season four was released in two blocks.

(958) Believe it or not, despite the fact that Joyce has now adopted Eleven, the two characters only speak to each other for the first time in the finale The Piggyback.

(959) The abandoned mill in Stranger Things 3 is owned by

the Hess family.

(960) When Will Byers stares in the bathroom mirror at the end of season one, this is a reference to the end of the original run of Twin Peaks when Agent Cooper looked in the mirror and we saw that he had been infected with evil.

(961) Dr Owens orders a club sandwich. No prizes for guessing what Eleven orders. She requests waffles!

(962) The end of The Nina Project.

(963) True. Jennifer Fauveau was the female voice actor who dubbed Caleb McLaughlin into French.

(964) Dear Billy

(965) Jackson

(966) He completes a crossword.

(967) Matthew Modine turned down the part of Maverick in Top Gun. Tom Cruise was cast instead.

(968) The Muppet Movie

(969) Eleven has a picture of Mike in his Ghostbusters costume on her bedside table.

(970) Natalia Dyer

(971) Suzie, Do You Copy?

(972) Risotto

(973) The T-1000 'liquid' Terminator in Terminator 2: Judgment Day.

(974) Enola Holmes

(975) Eleven has made a little model of Hopper's cabin.

(976) When Dustin locates Dart in the school toilets in Stranger Things 2, you can see the word EVIL written on the wall.

(977) Noah Schnapp and Gaten Matarazzo.

(978) Ghostbusters II

(979) Agent Harmon and Agent Wallace.

(980) Pineapple on pizza.

(981) A recreational vehicle.

(982) He was pounced on by a Demogorgon.

(983) Nancy

(984) Jason Carver

(985) Terry Gilliam's Brazil

(986) Season two.

(987) Bob was going to be killed by the Flayer possessed Will.

(988) The rainbow room.

(989) Twice.

(990) The Creel House

(991) Noah Schnapp

(992) Amazingly, they said the wig actually cost $8,000!

(993) In second place was King's Landing from Game of

Thrones with 35% and in third place was Hogwarts with 22%.

(994) Dr Brenner wants Eleven to say she understands why he did all the things he did and agree that he only had her best interests at heart. Eleven declines to do this.

(995) Eleven plainly has some Reeboks in season three for the mall scenes. She also wears Converse elsewhere.

(996) A grandfather clock.

(997) Bob was supposed to die in episode two but the Duffers decided to keep Sean Astin around for longer because they were enjoying his performance.

(998) The scene in Raiders of the Lost Ark where Indiana Jones manages to obtain a German uniform in the Nazi U-boat base.

(999) Scarface with Al Pacino.

(1000) The Talisman by Stephen King and Peter Straub

9 798215 487143